ASTOC ARCHITECTS AND PLANNERS

JOVIS

⌐PORTFOLIO⌐

ASTOC ARCHITECTS AND PLANNERS

ULF MEYER

Herausgegeben von Edited by
Falk Jaeger

JOVIS

Alle vorgestellten Projekte sind mit Koordinaten versehen, die es erlauben, die Standorte der Gebäude z.B. über GoogleEarth exakt zu lokalisieren. For all projects presented coordinates are provided allowing the exact localisation of the buildings via GoogleEarth or other applications. © 2011 by jovis Verlag GmbH I Das Copyright für die Texte liegt bei den Autoren. Das Copyright für die Abbildungen liegt bei den Fotografen/Inhabern der Bildrechte. Texts by kind permission of the authors. Pictures by kind permission of the photographers/holders of the picture rights. Die Gesamtreihe Portfolio wird herausgegeben von Falk Jaeger The series Portfolio is edited by Falk Jaeger I Umschlagfoto Cover: vorn front H.G. Esch, hinten back Christa Lachenmaier I Alle Renderings, Zeichnungen, Abbildungen und Pläne sind von All renderings, sketches, illustrations, and drawings by ASTOC/KCAP Architects & Planners/Hamburgplan 8, 9, 12 (l.), 13 (l., m.), 17 (l.), 18 (l.) I ASTOC/MESS/BKSP 122 I ASTOC/MESS 123 I ASTOC Architects and Planners 124 (r.), 125, 129 (r.), 131 (r.) I ASTOC/RMP/Landschaft Planen und Bauen/Post und Welters 126, 127 I ASTOC/HPP Hentrich – Petschnigg & Partner 128 (l.) I ASTOC/GWJ 130 I ASTOC/R+T 131 (l.) I Sichtvision 128 (r.), 129 (l.) I Fotos Photographs ASTOC/KCAP Architects & Planners/Hamburgplan 12 (r.), 13 (r.) I ASTOC Architects and Planners 59 I Guido Baselgia 83, 84, 85, 87, 88, 89 I Jan Bitter 124 (l.) I ELBE&FLUT, Quelle: HafenCity Hamburg GmbH 16 (l., m.), 17 (r.), 18 (r.), 19, 20, 21 (l.) I H.G. Esch 26, 27, 28, 30, 31, 32, 34, 36, 37, 38, 39, 40, 42, 43, 44, 45, 90, 97, 98, 99 I Fotofrizz, Quelle: HafenCity Hamburg GmbH 16 (r.) I Geodaten: © Stadt Solingen · Der Oberbürgermeister · Stadtdienst Vermessung und Kataster (2011-2028) 64 I T. Kraus, Quelle: HafenCity Hamburg GmbH 21 (r.) I Christa Lachenmaier 46, 47, 48, 49, 51, 52, 53, 54, 56, 57, 69, 71, 72, 76, 77, 78, 80, 81, 93, 94, 95, 100, 103, 105, 106, 107, 108, 109, 110, 111, 113, 114, 115, 116, 117, 119, 132, 134, 138, 139, 140, 141, 142, 143, 144 I Günter Lintl 60, 62, 63, 65 I Manos Meisen 55 I Ulrich Neikes 75 I Sven Otte 66, 67 I Alle Rechte vorbehalten. All rights reserved. I Redaktionelle Mitarbeit Co-editing Ingo Kanehl, Markus Kersting, Prof. Markus Neppl, ASTOC Architects and Planners I Übersetzung Translation Julian Jain, Berlin I English proofreading Rachel Hill, London I Gestaltung und Satz Design and setting Susanne Rösler, Berlin I Lithografie Lithography Bild1Druck, Berlin I Druck und Bindung Printing and binding GCC Grafisches Centrum Cuno, Calbe I Bibliografische Information der Deutschen Nationalbibliothek Bibliographic information published by Die Deutsche Nationalbibliothek Die Deutsche Nationalbibliothek verzeichnet diese Publikation in der Deutschen Nationalbibliografie; detaillierte bibliografische Daten sind im Internet über http://dnb.d-nb.de abrufbar. Die Deutsche Nationalbibliothek lists this publication in the Deutsche Nationalbibliografie; detailed bibliographic data are available in the Internet at http://dnb.d-nb.de jovis Verlag GmbH I Kurfürstenstraße 15/16 I 10785 Berlin I www.jovis.de I ISBN 978-3-86859-117-0

INHALT
CONTENTS

VORWORT
PREFACE

Falk Jaeger

Es waren die Heroen der Moderne wie Walter Gropius, Otto Haesler und vor allem Ludwig Hilberseimer, die Le Corbusiers Diktum von der Ville Radieuse konsequent weiter, ja zu Ende dachten und städtebauliche Entwürfe von höchster Stringenz und kühlster Rationalität veröffentlichten und zum Teil sogar realisierten. Ausgehend von Forderungen nach kostendrückender Rationalisierung des Bauwesens war für sie der Zeilenbau die Lösung des Wohnungsproblems der Weimarer Republik sowie ein Weg zur Behebung sozialer Missstände durch Bereitstellung gesunder, menschenwürdiger Behausungen mit Licht, Luft und Sonne.

Erst viel später, zu spät, begriff man, dass die Freiflächen zwischen den Zeilen zum unbrauchbaren Abstandsgrün degenerierten und dass die Zeilenarchitektur mit den optimierten Wohnungsgrundrissen den Virus der Monotonie in sich trug. Noch der Wiederaufbau der fünfziger Jahre ließ sich von der Idee der Charta von Athen begeistern. Und als in den sechziger Jahren die großen Bauträger das Ruder in die Hand nahmen, waren die Architekten ganz trunken von den gebotenen Möglichkeiten und lieferten willfährig im Maßstab 1:5000 geplante Trabantenstädte immer nach dem Schema Baukörper mit seriellen Wohnungen eingebettet in neutralem, das heißt eigenschaftslosem Abstandsgrün.

Seitdem ist Arbeit an der Überwindung der hundert Jahre alten Planungsphilosophie gefragt, deren Produkte Zeilenbau und Großsiedlung waren. ASTOCs städtebauliches Agieren ist allzeit von dem Bewusstsein geprägt, dass die Entwicklung urbaner Strukturen nicht das Werk eines Demiurgen ist, der die materielle Welt nach seinem Gutdünken gestaltet, sondern dass eine Vielzahl von Handelnden sich zusammenfinden müsse, um zu einem gesellschaftlich sanktionierten Ergebnis zu kommen. Städtebau ist zuerst Abwägen von Einzelideen und -interessen. Die urban aktive, abwechslungsreiche, allen Bewohnern und Nutzern zugetane Lebenswelt kann nach Überzeugung von ASTOC nur auf solche Weise entstehen.

Überwinden will ASTOC auch die Lücke in der Denkweise zwischen Architektur und Stadtplanung, zwischen der objektorientierten Arbeit und der langfristigen, manchmal langatmigen, sagen wir positiver, den langen Atem erfordernden Planung im städtischen Kontext. Es bedarf des Engagements für Qualität auf allen Ebenen, Engagement, das sich dem Automatismus selbstlaufender, weil ökonomischer Prozesse entgegenstemmt. Wenn die Verhältnisse die Vereinzelung der Planer innerhalb eines städtebaulichen Entwicklungsprozesses bewirken – die Stadt sucht den Investor, der Investor ordert eine Planung und gleichzeitig einen Generalunternehmer, Architekten für die Einzelobjekte, einen Landschaftsplaner für die Freiflächen und findet einen Betreiber der Infrastruktur – so gilt es, die Automatismen der Verhältnisse zu durchbrechen, im Entstehungsprozess frühzeitig einzusteigen und die Zügel in der Hand zu behalten, im Fall von ASTOC idealerweise vom Gewinn des städtebaulichen Wettbewerbs bis zur Schlüsselübergabe.

Dazu muss man sich auf allen relevanten Feldern als kompetent erweisen und im Zweifelsfall schlicht besser sein als die anderen Agierenden. Es läge nahe, im eigenen Büro mit Experten aus verschiedenen Fachrichtungen ein interdisziplinäres Planungsteam aufzustellen, um zu den angestrebten gesamtheitlichen Planungsergebnissen zu gelangen. Doch ASTOC will bewusst keine Paketlösungen intern erarbeiten. Je nach Charakter der vorliegenden Aufgaben werden Kooperationen mit Fachleuten anderer Disziplinen angestrebt, immer neu und immer maßgeschneidert, um immer neue Anregungen und Ideen einarbeiten zu können. Aus dieser Überzeugung erwächst ein ganzheitliches Verständnis der Gestaltung unserer Umwelt, wie es heute nur wenige Architektur- und Stadtplanungsbüros an den Tag legen.

It was the heroes of modernity of the likes of Walter Gropius, Otto Haesler, and Ludwig Hilberseimer in particular who systematically continued and even thought through Le Corbusier's dictum of the Ville Radieuse, publicizing some of the most rigorous and severely rational urban plans ever, which were, in certain cases, even implemented. Taking the demands for a cost-cutting rationalization of the building sector as their starting point these architects saw row-type housing as the ideal solution to the housing problem of the Weimar Republic, addressing various social grievances by providing healthy and humane dwellings with adequate natural and artificial light and ventilation.

It was only much later, too late actually, that it became painfully apparent that the open spaces between the rows had degenerated into unusable and sterile green "buffer zones" and that the row-type architecture with its optimized apartment floor plans were leading to little else than crass monotony. Even the post-war reconstruction of the nineteen-fifties still displayed a fascination for the ideas of the Athens Charter. When large real estate developers took over in the sixties, architects were only too eager to oblige them with compliant plans for new satellite cities. Depicted in the ubiquitous scale of 1:5000, these plans all adhered to the dictum of constructing monolithic apartment building blocks with standardized apartments set in a neutral, i.e. faceless, green buffer zone.

Ever since, it has taken a great deal of effort to overcome this hundred-year-old planning philosophy which had led to these row-type apartment blocks and large housing estates. ASTOC's urban planning endeavors are constantly shaped by the realization that the development of urban structures is not the result of the actions of a demiurge who may only be concerned with designing the material world to fit his own subjective precepts, but of a communicative process involving a large number of actors who come together to create a socially sanctioned result. Urban planning first and foremost has to do with the process of assessing individual ideas and interests. It is only in this way that an actively urban and varied atmosphere that is equally attractive for all residents can come about, as ASTOC firmly believes.

The firm strives to close the gap between the thought patterns of architects and those of urban planners, between object-oriented work and the long-term (and sometimes lengthy) process of planning in an urban context. What is needed is commitment to quality on all levels and a dedication that counters the seemingly automated nature of economic processes. If conditions are such that they induce various actors to produce only isolated and excessively individualistic results within an urban development framework, conventionally running through normative procedures such as a city's search for investors, the commissioning of an urban plan, the search for a general contractor by the investor, the commissioning of architects for individual buildings and that of landscape planners for open spaces, and the search for an operator of the infrastructure, an extra effort has to be made to break through this mundane façade of conventional processes. The goal ought rather to be to intervene in the developmental process at an early stage, thereby retaining control of it. In ASTOC's case, this would ideally include all the planning stages from a competition success down to the hand-over of keys of new buildings.

To be able to do this, competency in all relevant fields is required, in many cases calling for greater competency than that of the other involved actors. One way to achieve this is to bring together experts from a wide range of fields in the office itself, setting up an interdisciplinary planning team that can arrive at the intended holistic planning goals. At the same time, ASTOC don't want their internal office-based efforts to lead to predetermined "package solutions". Depending on the character of the tasks at hand, customized cooperation with experts from other fields is encouraged to be able to include new inputs and ideas. This conviction leads to a holistic understanding of the design of our surroundings and of our environment, an approach that only few architecture and urban planning firms are capable of seeing through.

GEMESSENE SCHRITTE – STRATEGIEN FÜR HAUS, STADT UND REGION
MEASURED STEPS—STRATEGIES FOR BUILDINGS, CITIES, AND REGIONS

Andreas Denk

„Wenn Du ein Haus baust, denke an die Stadt"[1]: Luigi Snozzis einprägsamer Aphorismus scheint wie kaum ein anderes Theorem allgemeine Bedeutung für die Architektur unserer Zeit zu haben – und sogar darüber hinaus zu deuten. Jenseits aller stilistischen Fragen, so lässt sich Snozzis Sentenz verstehen, soll das Ergebnis des Bauprozesses – im besten Falle

„Eindrücke", die wir als „Stadtbild", als „Milieu" oder als „Anspruchsniveau" wahrnehmen. Jeder neue Hausbau, jeder neue „Eindruck" also, verändert oder bestätigt das Bild, das Milieu oder das Anspruchsniveau seiner unmittelbaren Umgebung, seines Quartiers oder sogar der gesamten Stadt: Jedes Mal treffen Bauherr und Architekt mit der Wahl des Erschei-

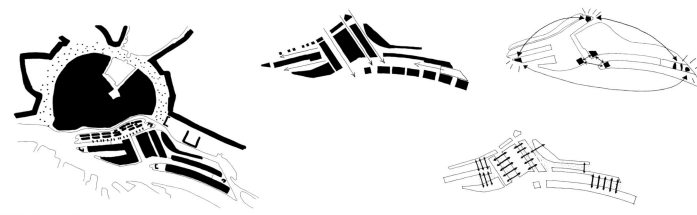

DIE HAFENCITY ALS ERWEITERUNG DER HAMBURGER INNENSTADT THE HAFENCITY AS EXTENSION OF HAMBURG'S INNER CITY MASSENVERTEILUNG, SICHTACHSEN DISTRIBUTION OF BUILDING MASSES; LINES OF SIGHT VERBINDUNGEN CONNECTIONS ÜBERGEORDNETE ATTRAKTOREN PRIMARY ATTRACTORS

„Architektur" – immer so konzipiert sein, dass es ein Teil des übergeordneten Kontinuums Stadt werden kann. Dient das Haus den Zwecken Einzelner oder einer Gruppe, so ist die Stadt der Ausdruck der Gesamtheit ihrer Bürger und ihrer gesellschaftlichen Verfasstheit. Auf beiden Ebenen wird Architektur zum Ausdruck der spezifischen Gesellungsformen des Menschen. Nimmt man den Begriff des „Ausdrucks" wörtlich, so wird er zum „Eindruck": Die Räumlichkeit und das Relief des einzelnen Bauwerks drücken sich dem öffentlichen Raum ein. Die Ansammlung von verschiedenen oder ähnlichen Häusern erzeugt viele verschiedene oder viele ähnliche

nungsbildes „ihres" Hauses eine Entscheidung über Autonomie oder Dependenz, über die Eigenwilligkeit oder die Anpassungsfähigkeit des Auftritts eines Gebäudes im öffentlich wahrnehmbaren Kontext.

Snozzis Satz legt nahe, die Wirkmächtigkeit von Bauwerken sehr sorgfältig zu betrachten und die entsprechenden Mittel sehr behutsam zu verwenden. Denn dient das Haus zuallererst den Zwecken Einzelner oder einer Gruppe, so soll es – richtig verstanden – fernerhin zum Wohle aller beitragen. Neben der individuellen Repräsentation, die Gebäuden durch ihre „Eindrücklichkeit" immer innewohnt, sollen sie, so ist Snozzi zu interpretieren, die Aufgabe

"Think of the city when you are building a house."[1] Luigi Snozzi's catchy aphorism, like no other perhaps, seems to fit especially well to the architecture of our times. It can even be understood to transcend the immediate field of architecture. Snozzi's statement illustrates that beyond pure issues of style, generic building processes (that may deserve to be called "milieus," or as "aspiration levels." Every new building, and with it, every new "impression," changes or confirms these images, these milieus or aspiration levels of its immediate surroundings, its quarter, or even of the whole city it is part of: every time architects and clients endeavor to construct a building, thereby having to choose a visual language for it,

HAFENCITY HAMBURG: WETTBEWERBSMODELL HAFENCITY HAMBURG: COMPETITION ENTRY MODEL | HAFENCITY HAMBURG: MASTERPLAN 2000 HAFENCITY HAMBURG: MASTER-PLAN 2000

"architecture" in certain cases) ought to be planned to become a part of the overriding continuum of the city. While buildings serve the purposes of specific individuals or groups, the city is an expression of all its citizens and of its complex social constitution. On both levels, architecture turns into the expression of specific social affiliations of human beings. Understanding the term "expression" literally makes it turn into "impression." The spatial quality and profile of an individual building makes an impression on public space. A collection of diverse or even similar buildings produces many different or many similar "impressions" that we perceive as "urban images", as what they are actually engaging in is deciding over questions of autonomy and dependency, of originality and adaptability of its appearance in a public context.

Snozzi's statement invites us to carefully study the efficacy of buildings and to utilize resources of space and the perception of space very cautiously. Even if buildings primarily serve the purposes of certain individuals or groups, an effort ought to be made to allow them to contribute to the larger good of the city. Apart from a building's individual representation that every building by default has on account of its "impressibility," it should, according to Snozzi, strive

haben, sich zum baulichen Ausdruck der Gesamtheit der Stadtbevölkerung in Beziehung zu setzen, sich in die Stadt einzufügen und sie zu bereichern. Bei aller Individualität der Nutzung und Gestaltung soll das Gebäude doch das Gemeinschaftliche der Stadt wahrnehmen, achten, ja verstärken. Diese naheliegende Betrachtung rechtfertigt, dass eine Reihe von Architekten und Stadtplanern auch heute noch davon spricht, dass Architektur und Städtebau von einer gesellschaftlichen Verantwortung getragen werden – und keineswegs nur als Ware, als Investitionsgut oder als Produkt einer Dienstleistung zu verstehen sind.

Der „uomo universale" Leon Battista Alberti hat in seinem Traktat *De re aedificatoria* 1485 davon gesprochen, dass das Haus wie eine Stadt, die Stadt aber wie ein Haus zu betrachten sei.[2] Albertis organischer Ansatz lässt sich heute so verstehen, dass wir genauso, wie wir die Zimmer eines Hauses mit aller Sorgfalt einrichten, damit sie als Zuhause dienen können, auch die Teile der Stadt auffassen sollten: Wie das Haus und seine Zimmer benötigen die Stadt und ihre Teile Liebe, Sorgfalt und kontinuierliche Pflege, damit sie zu einer „Wohnung" werden können. Diese Erkenntnis könnte der Ausgangspunkt der Arbeit des Kölner Städtebau- und Architekturbüros ASTOC Architects and Planners gewesen sein: Betrachtet man die Strategien und Methoden der Kölner Architekten seit der Gründung durch Peter Berner, Kees Christiaanse, Oliver Hall und Markus Neppl im Jahre 1990, so erkennt man in den differenzierten Arbeitsbereichen, die das notwendigerweise pragmatische Wirken in verschiedenen Maßstäben der Planung mit sich bringt, immer noch den idealistischen Kern des Ansatzes des Büros: ASTOC versteht das Phänomen der Stadt zwar nicht – wie Snozzi oder Alberti – als feststehende Größe oder gegebene formale Einheit, sondern im Anschluss an eine in den 1990er Jahren insbesondere in den Niederlanden ausformulierte Stadttheorie als sich ständig veränderndes Abbild eines kontinuierlichen Veränderungsprozesses. Diese Auffassung der „Stadt" als eines – am besten wohl filmhaft dar- und vorstellbaren – dynamischen

Transformationsprozesses, an dem eine mitunter große Zahl von „Akteuren" – Bauherren, Investoren, Projektentwickler, Beamte, Politiker, Bürger – mit unterschiedlichen Interessen teilnimmt, macht die Arbeit an der Stadt dennoch nicht beliebig. Vielmehr führt dieses prozessuale Denken der Stadt zu einer hochkomplexen Betrachtungsform, die neben den klassischen räumlich-formalen Gestaltungsparametern zeitliche, soziologische, wirtschaftliche und politische Aspekte integriert. Die Gestaltung der Stadt, so hat es ASTOC kürzlich formuliert, muss gezielt und kontinuierlich beeinflusst werden. „Komplexe Bezüge zwischen kleinräumigen, strategischen Eingriffen und großflächigen Funktionszusammenhängen erfordern anpassungsfähige räumliche Konzepte. Ziel ist eine prozesshafte Begleitung und Steuerung städtebaulicher Projekte, die eine Verknüpfung mit bestehenden Strukturen ermöglicht".[3]

Soll dieser Spagat zwischen übergreifender Planung und punktueller Intervention, zwischen dem Entwurf im stadtplanerischen Maßstab und dem bis ins Detail entworfenen Gebäude gelingen, wachsen die Ansprüche an die Qualität und die Leistungsfähigkeit eines Büros. Nicht das komplexe Denken, das komplexe Entwerfen allein hilft dann. Verlangt ist genauso das variantenreiche Springen zwischen verschiedenen Entwurfsebenen, die nicht nur intellektuell, sondern auch arbeitsorganisatorisch gefasst werden müssen. So ergeben sich aus städtebaulichen Rahmenplänen zwangsläufig bestimmte Parameter für die Gebäude, die sie ausfüllen sollen. Dabei kann es nützlich sein, für die Architektur – also für den Umgang mit der Stadt – bestimmte, nicht zu allgemeine und nicht zu strenge Codices zu entwickeln, die die gewünschte Entwicklung ermöglichen, aber nicht behindern sollen. Und andersherum können aus der architektonischen Praxis Erkenntnisse für die Spezifizierung von Gestaltungs- und Masterplänen erwachsen, die auf einer rein städtebaulichen Betrachtungsebene niemals zum Ziel der Betrachtung geworden wären. Dazu ist ein flexibles Arbeiten in möglichst „interdisziplinär" besetzten Teams und Gruppen nötig, die jeweils nach Größe und Besonderheit der

to find a place for itself in relation to the built expression of the entire urban society, endeavoring to fit into the city, thereby enriching it. However much it may be individualistic in its use and design, a building ought to take notice of what is common to a city, which it ought to honor and preferably even actively strengthen with its own architecture. This seemingly obvious observation explains the fact that a number of architects and urban planners today still talk of architecture and urban planning as having a wider social responsibility, believing that they should, under no circumstances, be considered to be generate mundane "products," investment goods or services only.

The "uomo universale" Leon Battista Alberti, suggested in his 1485 treatise *De re aedificatoria* that a building be understood as a city, and a city be understood as a building.[2] Alberti's organic approach can today be taken to prompt us to perceive the individual parts of a city as we perceive those of a house. Just like a building with its spaces and rooms, the city (and its parts) is itself a dwelling, requiring love, care, and continued maintenance. This fundamental realization may very well have represented the starting point of the work of the Cologne-based urban planning and architecture firm ASTOC Architects and Planners. The firm was founded by Peter Berner, Kees Christiaanse, Oliver Hall and Markus Neppl in 1990. While its varied body of work is pragmatically suited to allow for the handling of different planning scales, the idealistic core of the firm's approach is evident at all times: although ASTOC don't view the phenomenon of the city as being fixed in scale or formal unity, like Snozzi or Alberti had, they do perceive the city as a continually changing image of a repeated transformation process, alluding to an urbanism theory that was particularly influential in the Netherlands in the nineteen-nineties. At the same time, this perception of the city, representing an almost film-like dynamic transformation process, occasionally involving a large number of diverse "actors" such as clients, investors, project developers, civil servants, politicians, and citizens, should not

be understood as producing random results only. Rather, process-oriented thought leads to a highly complex observation method that integrates not just conventional spatial-formal design parameters, but also temporal, sociological, economic and political aspects. As ASTOC has recently stated, the design of the city needs to be continuously shaped and reshaped. "Complex references involving small-scale, strategic interventions and large-scale functional interrelations require adaptable spatial concepts. Our goal is to apply process-led supervision and guidance of urban planning projects, allowing them to connect with existing concepts and structures."[3]

If the balancing act between interdisciplinary planning and point-wise intervention, i.e. between designs on the scale of a city and those on the scale of buildings is to succeed, an architecture and planning firm must be able to live up to the heightened expectations that these conditions demand. What is needed is not just complex thinking but complex designing. Equally required is flexible and effortless movement between different design levels that need to be intellectually and organizationally structured. Urban planning frameworks, for example, are one type of structuring tool, inevitably resulting in certain overriding building parameters. In doing so, it can be useful to develop specific directives for the architecture and its treatment of the city, that are neither too strict nor too general, having the potential to lead to desired developments while still remaining flexible. In turn, architectural insights can lead to improved specifications for master-plans and design plans which otherwise would never command attention on a purely urban planning level. This requires flexible work practices, most preferably in interdisciplinary teams and groups that can be brought together according to the size and particularity of the task and the skills of the employees, being complemented by further specialists if required. This working method is characteristic of ASTOC: with currently forty-five employees, and the managing directors Peter Berner, Oliver Hall, Ingo Kanehl, Andreas Kühn, Markus Neppl and Jörg Ziolkowski as heads, the firm believes in

Aufgabe und der Fähigkeiten der Bearbeiter zusammengestellt und gegebenenfalls um Spezialisten ergänzt werden können. Diese Arbeitsweise ist ein Charakteristikum von ASTOC: Die Bürostruktur zielt mit derzeit 45 Mitarbeitern und Peter Berner, Oliver Hall, Ingo Kanehl, Andreas Kühn, Markus Neppl und Jörg Ziolkowski in der Geschäftsleitung sehr präzise auf die innerhalb der Arbeitsgruppen gleichmäßig verteilte Beherrschung aller unterschiedlichen Entwurfsebenen ab.[4]

Beispielhaft für die Arbeitsweise der Kölner Architekten und Stadtplaner ist die Entwicklung und städtebauliche Konkretisierung des Masterplans für die Hamburger HafenCity. Das Mammutprojekt – das

baulicher Einheiten untergliedert, andererseits durch sie miteinander verbunden. Die abstrakte strukturelle oder besser: die konzeptuelle Ebene soll der Masterplan für die HafenCity jedoch nicht überschreiten. Denn ASTOC versteht seinen Masterplan gewissermaßen als Gegenentwurf zu den hergebrachten stadtbaulichen Planfestlegungen. In einem Text von Markus Neppl zum „Bauen in Hafengebieten" klingt deutliche Kritik an der vielfach geübten Stadtplanungspraxis an: „Die Strategie vieler Kommunen, sich aufgrund fehlender Mittel aus der aktiven Planung zurückzuziehen und die Realisierung ganzer Stadtviertel professionellen Entwicklern zu überlassen, geht oft nicht auf. Die gebauten Ergebnisse blei-

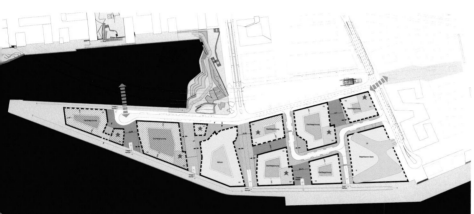 

HAFENCITY HAMBURG: FUNKTIONSPLAN STRANDKAI HAFENCITY HAMBURG: FUNCTIONAL PROGRAM OF THE STRANDKAI

größte dieser Jahre in Europa – wurde 1999 mit einem Wettbewerb eingeleitet, den das Team ASTOC/ Kees Christiaanse/Hamburgplan für sich entschied. Vom Sandtorhafen im Westen reicht das Masterplangebiet entlang des nördlichen Elbufers bis zum östlichen Baakenhafen – eine Fläche von 150 Hektar, auf denen bis 2030 Wohnraum für etwa 12.000 Menschen und 40.000 Arbeitsplätze entstehen sollen. Die block-, winkel- und hakenförmigen Strukturen, die das gesamte Gebiet überziehen, sind in mehreren städtebaulichen Clustern mit unterschiedlichen Körnungsgrößen zusammengefasst und durch parkähnlich konzipierte Freiflächen einerseits in städte-

ben oft fragmentarisch und haben mit den schönen Bildern aus den ursprünglichen Planungen nicht viel zu tun." Das liege daran, dass städtebauliche Pläne oftmals als „stabile Gerüste" beschrieben würden, die mit so genannten Platzhaltern ausgefüllt sind. Räumliche Qualität werde vor allem anhand der Ausgestaltung des öffentlichen Raums beurteilt, wohingegen „architektonische Fragen konsequent ausgeblendet" würden. „Wenn diese Planwerke dann die rechtlichen und ökonomischen Prozeduren durchlaufen haben, bleibt von den ursprünglichen Zielen nicht viel übrig".[5] Der HafenCity-Masterplan hingegen versuche nicht, ein „einmal entworfenes Bild

evenly spreading different competencies that relate to all design process levels within various working groups.[4]

The development and finalization of the master-plan for Hamburg's HafenCity represents a good example of the working method of the Cologne-based firm. The mammoth project, the largest in Europe in recent times, was initiated in 1999 following a competition which was won by the team of ASTOC, Kees Christiaanse, and Hamburgplan. The master-planned site extends from the Sandtorhafen in the west along the northern bank of the Elbe River to the Baakenhafen in the east, covering an area of 150 hectares where housing for approximately 12,000 people and

a strategy of withdrawing from active planning processes citing a lack of funds, thereby leaving the realization of entire urban quarters to professional developers, which, in many cases, just doesn't work. The built-form often appears fragmented, having little to do with the pretty pictures presented in the original plans." The reason for this grievance allegedly lies in the practice of defining urban plans as "sturdy scaffoldings" that are to be "filled out" by "placeholders." Also, spatial quality is often judged by the design of the public spaces only, systematically ignoring "questions that are of architectural importance." "Once these plans have gone through the grind of making them legally and economically

HAFENCITY HAMBURG: ÜBERSEEQUARTIER HAFENCITY HAMBURG: OVERSEAS QUARTER | FUNKTIONSPLAN ÜBERSEEQUARTIER FUNCTIONAL PROGRAM OF THE OVERSEAS QUARTER | WORKSHOP ZUR ÜBERARBEITUNG DES BEBAUUNGSKONZEPTES WORKSHOP FOR THE REVISION OF THE BUILDING CONCEPT

40,000 new jobs are to be created by 2030. The oblong, angular and hook-shaped structures covering the entire site are grouped into several urban clusters with varying scales and densities, and divided into urban planning units by park-like open spaces which also serve to connect them with each other. At the same time, the master-plan of the HafenCity strives to retain a crucially important abstract structural and conceptual dimension. This is because ASTOC understands its master-plan as an alternative to conventional urban plans. In his writing Building in Harbor Areas, Markus Neppl criticizes existing urban planning practice: "Many municipalities adopt

acceptable, there is not much left of the original goals."[5] In contrast, the master-plan of the HafenCity avoids the folly of "clinging on to a singular, preconceived image that it wants to blindly force through." The plan's underlying framework, as ASTOC understands it, is actually a behavioral code for all actors involved in the planning of the harbor areas. "Apart from the planning and economic instruments, it is the manner and type of communication in particular that finally determines the quality of a project."[6]

The first built result of these work-intensive efforts to find common urban and architectural ground can be seen at the Sandtorhafen, completed in 2010,

zu fixieren und dann mit Gewalt und Restriktionen durchzusetzen". Das Regelwerk des Plans, wie ihn ASTOC versteht, ist vielmehr ein Verhaltenskodex für alle Akteure, die an der Planung der Hafenquartiere beteiligt sind: „Es sind neben den planerischen und ökonomischen Instrumenten vor allem die Umgangsformen und die Art und Weise der Kommunikation, welche die Qualität eines Plans letztendlich bestimmen".[6]

Das erste Resultat dieser arbeitsreichen Bemühungen um einen gemeinsamen städtebaulichen und architektonischen Nenner ist die 2010 abgeschlossene architektonische Gestaltung des Sandtorhafens, zu dem auch ASTOC Architects and Planners mit ihrem Wohngebäude auf dem Baufeld 4 einen baulichen Beitrag geleistet hat. Trotz des unverkennbaren Wunsches aller beteiligten Architekten nach großer individueller Autonomie hat man sich auf eine architektonische Sprache verständigt, die dem erweiterten Formenkanon der Moderne entnommen ist. Fast alle Architekten haben sich an das gewünschte Bauvolumen gehalten, fast allen war der gemeinschaftliche Auftritt ähnlich wichtig wie das marketingträchtige „Alleinstellungsmerkmal" einer besonders auffälligen und von allen Nachbarn unterscheidbaren Architektur. Am Sandtorhafen ist ein stadträumliches Erlebnisfeld mit vergleichsweise hoher architektonischer Qualität entstanden, das spätere Jahrzehnte im Vergleich zu anderen Großplanungen unserer Zeit möglicherweise als Versuch eines einheitlichen Städtebaus und als filigranes Spiel mit Varianten einer architektonischen Typologie charakterisieren werden. Ähnliche Beharrlichkeit, Geduld und langer Atem wird auch bei der weiteren Entwicklung des großen Masterplans für die Berliner Heidestraße – nördlich des Hauptbahnhofs – vonnöten sein, den ASTOC seit dem Wettbewerbsgewinn 2008 bearbeitet. Hier sollen in den nächsten Jahren auf 40 Hektar 600.000 Quadratmeter Fläche für Büros, Wohnen, Kultur und Freizeit entstehen.[7]

Wie flexibel die Architekten eine grundlegende Idee handhaben können, zeigt ein weiteres Hafenprojekt ASTOCs – die Planung des Hamburger Holzhafens.

Hier hatten ASTOC/Kees Christiaanse im Jahre 2000 einen Wettbewerb um zwei Bürogebäude gewonnen. Durch die Weiterentwicklung des Projekts wurden daraus zwei veränderte Bürogebäude und ein Wohnturm. Die Bürobauten haben die Architekten im Format des klassischen hanseatischen Kontorhauses siebengeschossig angelegt und – voneinander leicht differierend – so mit mäanderförmig gegeneinander versetzten Geschossen ausgelegt, dass jede Büroeinheit Blick auf die Elbe hat. Das dritte Gebäude sollte ursprünglich den Gestaltungsparadigmen der beiden Bürohäuser folgen. Die besondere Lage des Geländes schien den Architekten indes so wertvoll, dass sie im Zusammenwirken mit dem Bauherrn und der städtischen Baubehörde von der ursprünglichen Planung abgewichen sind. Statt eines weiteren Baublocks schlug ASTOC einen Wohnturm zwischen den beiden Ziegelbauten vor, der sich auf einem Sockelgeschoss als prismatisch wirkender, zweiarmiger Turm mit einer elementierten Doppelfassade entwickelt.[8] Das Projekt zeigt, welche Wirkung das kooperative Vorgehen von Architekten, Bauherren und genehmigender Behörde erzielen kann. Der Aufwand und der Mut, die die Neuplanung erforderten, haben sich gelohnt: Schon vor der Fertigstellung sind die komfortablen und recht kostspieligen Apartments und Wohnungen des „Kristalls" zu einer höchst begehrten Hamburger Adresse geworden.

Die Veränderung des Gewohnten ist im allgemeinen Bewusstsein mit einem „Phantomschmerz" verbunden. Die unablässige und immer schnellere Transformation der Stadt überschreitet mitunter die Grenzen der Aufnahmefähigkeit und Toleranz der Menschen, die unter immer neuen räumlichen Bedingungen leben. Die Beschränkung dieser unvermeidlichen Verlusterfahrung sollte eigentlich Teil verantwortlicher Stadtentwicklungskonzepte sein. Wie gewohnte Strukturen zu erhalten und gleichzeitig zu verbessern sind, hat ASTOC bei der Konversion des Kernbestands der Siedlung Buchheimer Weg in Köln gezeigt.[9] Die Zeilenbausiedlung aus den 1950er Jahren macht etwa 20 Prozent des Kölner Stadtteils Ostheim aus. Ein Teil des nach gut 50 Jahren Nut-

where ASTOC Architects and Planners have built a residential building in the Baufeld 4 sector. In spite of all the involved architects' unequivocal desire to achieve a high degree of individual autonomy on the site, an architectural language that is derived from the extended formal canon of modernity, was agreed upon. Almost all architects have stuck to the desired floor space guidelines and also found it important to make a joint presentation of their concepts, creating unique architecture that is, at the same time, still clearly distinguishable from that of its neighbors. As such, the result is an urban space that allows for diverse experiences with comparatively high architectural quality. The interventions at the Sandtorhafen site may in future, and with hindsight, well be characterized as an ambitious attempt to create more holistic urban planning and delicate interplays of different variants of a specific architectural typology when compared to other current large-scale planning interventions.

Similar perseverance, patience and staying power will probably also be required for the further development of the large-scale master-plan for Berlin's Heidestrasse, north of the central station, a project ASTOC has been working on since its competition win in 2008. It is here that 600,000 square meters of office and housing space, as well as cultural and recreational space spread over 40 hectares are to be built over the next several years.[7]

How proficient and flexible ASTOC are at handling fundamentally important and innovative urban planning concepts is shown by another harbor project of theirs: the planning of Hamburg's Timber Harbor. ASTOC/Kees Christiaanse had won a competition to build two office buildings here in 2000. The further development of the project resulted in two modified office buildings and a residential tower. The architects laid out the office buildings in the format of classic Hanseatic office buildings (Kontorhäuser), being seven stories high and each slightly different from the other, with gently offset meandering floors, allowing each office unit to enjoy views of the Elbe River. The third building was originally planned to follow the design parameters of the two office buildings. The special location of the site, however, seemed so precious to the architects that they, in cooperation with the client and the municipal building authority, divulged from the original plan. Instead of building a further building block, ASTOC suggested building a residential tower between the two clinker buildings that would rest on a pedestal level as a prismatic double-winged tower with a module-like double facade.[8] The project wonderfully shows the positive impact that can be achieved by intensive cooperation between architects, the client and public authorities. The effort and the courage which the new planning required paid off in the end: even before completion, the comfortable and rather expensive apartments of the "crystal building" have become a highly prized residential address in Hamburg. In public consciousness, changing conventional behavior is generally associated with a kind of phantom pain. The ceaseless and ever-accelerating transformation of the city often transcends the limits of the absorbing capacity and tolerance of human beings who are obliged to adjust to constantly new living conditions. Keeping these seemingly inevitable losses within tolerable limits is ideally supposed to be an integral part of responsible city development concepts.

How familiar structures can be retained while simultaneously being upgraded, is exemplified by ASTOC's conversion of the existing building stock at the housing development of Buchheimer Weg in Cologne.[9] This row-type housing estate from the nineteen-fifties accounts for approximately twenty percent of the area of Cologne's Ostheim district. One part of the existing building stock that had begun to show its age after a good fifty years of use, had already been renovated by its owner, a housing association. For the western part of the complex multiple building assignments were commissioned in 2005. ASTOC won the competition procedure with the suggestion to completely replace the existing buildings by new ones, while retaining the underlying urban planning approach of the complex. However, instead of ada-

zung in die Jahre gekommenen Bestands war bereits von der Eigentümerin, einer Wohnungsbaugesellschaft, saniert worden. Für den westlichen Teil der Anlage sollte 2005 innerhalb einer Mehrfachbeauftragung eine weiterführende Lösung gefunden werden. ASTOC gewann das Verfahren mit einem Vorschlag, bei dem die Bestandsbauten zwar völlig durch Neubauten ersetzt wurden, jedoch die grundsätzliche städtebauliche Konzeption der Siedlung wieder aufgegriffen wurde. Statt der relativ beziehungslos zueinander stehenden Wohnzeilen konzipierten die Architekten etwas breitere, komfortablere und leicht geknickte Baukörper, die wahrnehmbare stadträumliche Kompartimente mit sinnfällig

wahl und architektonische Gestaltung der öffentlich geförderten Mehrfamilienhäuser im Rahmen des Angemessenen blieben. So ließ sich schließlich auch das soziale Milieu bewahren, das bei solchen Gelegenheiten allzu oft durch eine zu anspruchsvolle Attitüde überformt und zerstört wird. Ein ähnlicher Fall von „Bestandsschutz" war auch die Grube Carl in Frechen: Hier gelang es ASTOC zwischen 2005 und 2008, in Zusammenarbeit mit der zuständigen Denkmalpflegebehörde die zur Zeche gehörige Brikettfabrik so in Wohnungen umzubauen, dass der industrielle „Eindruck" der Gesamtanlage erhalten blieb, aber dennoch höchst originelle Wohnsituationen entstanden sind.[10]

HAFENCITY HAMBURG: FREIRÄUME DALMANNKAI HAFENCITY HAMBURG: OPEN SPACES AT DALMANNKAI | MARCO-POLO-TERRASSEN MARCO POLO TERRACES | MAGDEBURGER HAFEN, ÜBERSEEQUARTIER MAGDEBURG PORT, OVERSEAS QUARTER

definierten hofartigen Außenwohnräumen bilden. Die offenen und grünen Höfe haben einen hohen Wohnwert und geben eine gute Orientierung in der gesamten Siedlungsstruktur. Der Bestand an alten Bäumen, der den Charakter der Siedlung prägt, ist weitgehend erhalten worden und durch die Pflanzung weiterer Zierbäume und Hecken zum strukturierenden Element der differenzierten und zonierten Freiraumgestaltung des Geländes geworden. Doch blieben nicht nur die wesentlichen formalen Elemente der grundsätzlichen Gestaltung der Siedlung – in verbesserter Form – erkennbar. Vielmehr war den Architekten darüber hinaus wichtig, dass Material-

Für Kernbereiche von Städten werden nur selten Masterpläne entworfen. Hier geht es vielmehr um das Erkennen der Besonderheiten, Möglichkeiten und Schwächen des bestehenden städtischen Gewebes. Wie man eine komplexe Bauaufgabe mit der Festigung dieses Gewebes verbinden kann, zeigt das Projekt am Friesenplatz in Köln, das ASTOC zwischen 2008 und 2009 realisiert hat.[11] Ein seit seiner Entstehung am Anfang des letzten Jahrhunderts mehrfach umgebautes Büro- und Geschäftshaus mit vier aufeinander folgenden Hinterhäusern in der Kölner Innenstadt sollte aufgewertet und zu einer multifunktionalen Immobilie ausgebaut werden. Da-

mantly sticking to the seemingly random arrangement of the housing rows, the architects conceived broader, more comfortable and gently bent buildings that create tangible urban compartments with inviting courtyard-like exterior living spaces. The open, green courtyards offer a high living quality, also providing a good sense of orientation in the entire complex. Existing old trees that shape the character of the complex have been retained to the greatest extent possible while the planting of new ornamental trees and hedges has become an important structural element for creating a differentiated and zoned design of the open spaces on the site. At the same time, it was not only the valuable formal elements in such a way that the industrial character of the whole complex was not lost while allowing for new, highly original living spaces to be realized in collaboration with the relevant built heritage authority.[10] Rarely are master-plans drawn up for the core areas of cities; much more important for these areas is an understanding of particularities, possibilities and weaknesses of existing urban fabrics. ASTOC's project at Friesenplatz in Cologne (2008-09) shows how a complex building assignment can be interwoven with the consolidation of this urban fabric.[11] An office building with four successive rear buildings, dating from the beginning of the last century and modified several times, was to be upgraded and converted to

HAFENCITY HAMBURG: ÜBERARBEITUNG DES MASTERPLANS ÖSTLICHE HAFENCITY HAFENCITY HAMBURG: REVISION OF THE MASTER-PLAN FOR THE EASTERN HAFENCITY | TRADITIONSSCHIFFE IM SANDTORHAFEN TRADITIONAL TALL SHIPS AT SANDTORHAFEN

of the previous complex that were retained, albeit in much improved condition. Equally important for the architects was an appropriate choice of materials and the desire to allow the architecture of the publicly subsidized apartment buildings to fit to this particular situation. In this way, the social milieu of the area could be preserved which, in many other cases, is either forcibly converted or destroyed by an all-too-demanding formalist attitude.

The coal mine "Carl" in Frechen presented a similar case of protecting preexisting built-form: here, between 2005 and 2008, ASTOC succeeded in converting the mine's briquette factory into apartments multi-functional real estate. To serve this purpose, a low-key natural stone facade facing the street that recalls images of rationalist architecture was added. The rear buildings were reduced in number and decored, freeing up space for commercial activities on the basement levels and for apartments on the upper floors. The staggered arrangement of the unpretentious yet elegant courtyard facades equipped with loggias, balconies, and terraces, creates a true "living landscape" in this dense inner-city part of Cologne, beautifully reflecting the current trend towards ecologically, socially and economically re-appropriating inner city locations.

für bekam es zur Straße hin eine Natursteinfassade mit einem sehr zurückhaltenden Gliederungssystem, das wiederum Erinnerungen an rationalistische Architekturen wachruft. Die Hinterhäuser wurden reduziert und teilweise entkernt, sodass in den Untergeschossen Räume für Handel und Gewerbe, in den Obergeschossen aber Wohnräume eingerichtet werden konnten. Die Staffelung der unprätentiösen, aber elegant wirkenden Hoffassaden mit Loggien, Balkonen und Terrassen lässt hier in der dicht bebauten Kölner City eine regelrechte Wohnlandschaft entstehen, die dem Trend zur ökologisch, sozial und ökonomisch sinnvollen Rückkehr in die Innenstadt einen guten Ausdruck gibt.

tegien ASTOCs zurückwirken und wie das Büro die Konzeption von „Stadt" aus dem Kontinuum des Bestehenden, also aus der Kontinuität der städtischen Typologien heraus entwickelt. Die Erweiterungen des Rathauses und der Plan für die Unterstadt von Kleve[12], die Pläne für die Erweiterung der Abtei Hamborn oder die stadträumliche Gestalt, die ein Haltepunkt in Solingen bekommen hat, zeigen das Gespür für Strukturen und ihre Weiterverwertung oder Wiederaufnahme, die das Büro so auszeichnet.
Dabei sind es oftmals nicht nur die prestigeträchtigen klassischen Aufgaben, denen ASTOC sich mit Ernsthaftigkeit und Engagement widmet: Auch Gebäude, die banalen Zwecken der Infrastruktur dienen

HAFENCITY HAMBURG: ÜBERARBEITUNG DES MASTERPLANS ÖSTLICHE HAFENCITY HAFENCITY HAMBURG: REVISION OF THE MASTER-PLAN FOR THE EASTERN HAFENCITY | ERICUSSPITZE ERICUSSPITZE

Die Beispiele in Ostheim und am Friesenplatz belegen, wie sich die Bereiche der Planungs- und Entwurfstätigkeit von Architekten in der Gegenwart immer mehr Aufgaben zuwenden, die mit der Verdichtung, der Verbesserung, der Stabilisierung der bestehenden Stadt zu tun haben. In gewisser Weise scheint ASTOC bei solchen Projekten ihre stadträumlichen Masterplanmethoden – fast im Sinne Albertis – auf das einzelne Objekt zu übertragen, wenn sie die Entwicklungsmöglichkeiten und Potenziale eines Bestands kleinteilig analysiert und auslotet. Andererseits wird auch hier deutlich, wie die Erfahrungen der Arbeit im Bestand auf die großräumlichen Stra-

wie das Hochwasser-Pumpwerk an der Merkenicher Straße in Köln, das 2008 fertiggestellt wurde[13], beweist das Bemühen um die gute Gestaltung, das die „conditio sine qua non" des Architektenberufs ist. Der flache Bau in einem nahezu provisorischen Umfeld ist zur Metapher seiner Funktion geronnen: Über eine leicht geschwungene Basaltfassade rinnt gereinigtes Regenwasser, das über die Jahre die Natursteinwand in eine bemooste, weiche Fläche verwandeln wird – Sinnbild des besonderen Wertes, den Wasser für das Leben hat. Inzwischen gehört sogar ein ALDI-Supermarkt zu den Bauaufgaben, bei denen ASTOC versucht hat, eigentlich toten Ob-

The built examples at Ostheim and Friesenplatz exemplify how planning and design efforts by architects are increasingly geared towards densification and the improvement and stabilization of existing urban fabrics today. ASTOC succeeds in translating their urban master-planning approaches to individual buildings in projects such as this, thereby almost recalling Alberti's thought when considering how the firm minutely analyzes and gauges the developmental potential of existing building stocks in their work. Simultaneously, what this process also shows is how the engagement with existing building stock reflects back onto the large-scale strategies of ASTOC and how the firm develops its conception of "the

in 2008,[13] exemplifying the great deal of effort the architects and planners invest into producing good design, the "conditio sine qua non" of the architectural profession. The pumping station in Cologne is a flat building, located in rather provisionally-built surroundings. By virtue of its deign, it has become a metaphor of its own function: purified rainwater runs over a gently curved basalt facade, converting the natural stone wall into a moss-covered soft surface over the course of a few years, thereby symbolizing the special significance that water has for life. In the meanwhile, even an ALDI supermarket has become part of the firm's repertoire, a project where ASTOC have attempted to infuse life into rather life-

HAFENCITY HAMBURG: VASCO-DA-GAMA-PLATZ HAFENCITY HAMBURG: VASCO DA GAMA SQUARE | AM SANDTORPARK/GROSSER GRASBROOK AT THE SANDTOR-PARK/GROSSER GRASBROOK

city" from the continuity of existing stock, i.e. from the continuity of urban typologies. Projects such as the built extensions of the town hall and the plan for the lower town of the city of Kleve,[12] the plans for the extension of Hamborn Abbey or the urban gestalt of a public transport intersection in Solingen show the firm's flair for structures and their further use.
In doing so, ASTOC's repertoire is not limited to prestigious and classic assignments. The firm is also deeply committed to buildings with rather mundane purposes such as infrastructure projects that include the pumping station for flood water at Merkenicher Strasse in Cologne, completed

less built objects to the greatest extent possible.[14] Another assignment which is at least as challenging and considered hardly limitable in time, is the master-plan "Emscher Zukunft". A team comprising ASTOC/RMP Landscape Architects (Bonn), Landschaft Planen und Bauen (Berlin) and Post und Welters (Dortmund) were commissioned to work on this project following a 2003 competition win.[15] The format of the plan represents something entirely new in the firm's project history: it consists of a strip, eighty-five kilometers long, between Dinslaken and Dortmund-Holzwickede that forms the heart of ASTOC's concept of transforming the heteroge-

jekten ein Mindestmaß an architektonischem Leben einzuhauchen.[14]

Eine mindestens ebenso herausfordernde, ja: schwierige und zeitlich kaum eingrenzbare Aufgabenstellung ist der „Masterplan Emscher-Zukunft", dessen Bearbeitung das Team ASTOC/RMP Landschaftsarchitekten, Bonn/Landschaft Planen und Bauen, Berlin/Post und Welters, Dortmund als Ergebnis eines Wettbewerbs 2003 zugesprochen bekam.[15] Das Format des Plans ist im Werklauf des Kölner Büros bisher unerreicht: Er umfasst ein Band zwischen Dinslaken und Dortmund-Holzwickede. Auf einer Strecke von 85 Kilometern haben die Architekten für die sehr heterogenen Landschaftstei-

üblich, Impulse für neue Projekte geben und im Anschluss an diese grundsätzliche Verständigung über einen moderierten Prozess aller Planungsbeteiligten eine allmähliche Umsetzung der Kernidee des Masterplans möglich machen. Als Laufzeit des extensiv betriebenen Projekts sind deshalb 30 Jahre nicht zu gering angesetzt.

Bei Projekten dieses Maßstabs muten die Strategien und Methoden der Architekten auf den ersten Blick pragmatisch an, weil sie nicht große Bilder entwerfen, sondern Impulse geben und Mögliches moderieren. Diese gebotene Pragmatik sollte nicht darüber hinwegsehen lassen, dass all diesem Tun eine übergeordnete Vorstellung des gestalteten Ganzen

HAFENCITY HAMBURG: DIE QUEEN MARY II AM STRANDKAI HAFENCITY HAMBURG: THE 'QUEEN MARY II' AT THE STRANDKAI | DALMANNKAI DALMANNKAI

le und Städte des mittleren Ruhrgebiets ein „Neues Emschertal" in Aussicht genommen. Dabei soll der ökologische Umbau der ehemaligen kanalisierten Abwasserkloake, die das Revier in ost-westlicher Richtung durchläuft, als Ausgangspunkt für die Entwicklung des gesamten Ruhrgebiets dienen. Die „Neue Emscher" könnte, so erwarten die Architekten, zu einem „grünen Rückgrat für Freizeit und Kultur, für Wohnen und Arbeit" werden. Der Masterplan ist dabei mehr ein Verständigungsmittel für die sehr unterschiedlichen und mitunter westfälisch-eigensinnigen Akteure in den untereinander konkurrierenden Städten der Region: Er soll, wie bei ASTOC

zugrunde liegt. Diese Vorstellung, die unter den Architekten von ASTOC unumstritten ist, ist in der Tat insofern realitätsbezogen, indem sie die Komplexität menschlicher Interessen beim Bau des Gemeinwesens richtig einschätzt. Aber sie verleugnet deshalb nicht, dass sie das ideale Fernziel einer „guten Stadt" im Auge hat. Vielleicht lässt sich die Haltung des Büros als der immer erneuerte Versuch angemessenen Handelns verstehen: ASTOCs Ansatz geht von einer kontinuierlichen, nicht sprunghaften, sondern schrittweisen Veränderung der Stadt und ihrer Teile aus. Nichts anderes als die Fortschreibung der Stadt mit verbesserten Mitteln ist das Ziel der moderierten

neous landscapes and cities of the central Ruhr region into a new "Emscher Valley." In doing so, the ecological conversion of the former canalized waste-water sewer that runs through the area in an east-west direction has become the starting point for the further development of the entire Ruhr region. The "new Emscher" could become a "green spine for recreation and culture, housing and working," according to the architects. Thereby, the master-plan becomes more of a communication instrument for negotiating a diverse range of actors, including occasional Westphalian stubbornness, within the context of regionally competing cities: it was intended, as is the case in many ASTOC projects, to provide

that there very much is an underlying imaginary quality to all what is being designed. This understanding, undisputed among the architects at ASTOC, is indeed realistic insofar as it correctly assesses the complexity of human interests for an issue such as the creation of a sense of community. At the same time, it does not deny its long-term aim of bringing about "the good city." Perhaps the firm's posture can best be understood as representing the constantly renewed attempt to act in appropriate terms: ASTOC's approach exemplifies continual and gradual, not dramatic change of the city and its elements. The firm's moderated processes strive to give new life to the existing city. As such, "impressions" and

HAFENCITY HAMBURG: MAGELLAN-TERRASSEN HAFENCITY HAMBURG: MAGELLAN TERRACES | MARCO-POLO-TERRASSEN MARCO POLO TERRACES

fresh impulses for new projects, in keeping with this fundamental understanding of moderated processes that involve all persons concerned with the planning process, make possible a gradual implementation of the core idea of the master-plan. As such, a projected time period of thirty years does not seem unrealistic at all for this extensive project.

With projects of this scale, the strategies and methods employed by the architects may seem pragmatic at first sight, as they are not engaged with simply generating grand images, but rather provide innovative impulses and moderate possibilities. This sense of pragmatics should, however, not obscure the fact

"mouldings" should only gradually change like the corresponding urban planning typologies for the city to remain recognizable, in its constitution and gestalt and as living space and home. Therefore, the greatest effort ought to be invested into the improvement of existing architectural and urban planning repertoires. The repetition and hence the confirmation of the sense of "impression" by means of morphological reproduction and variation of time-tested types figures more prominently than the continuous invention of sensations and fancy novelties. Finally, it is not the individual, but the common good which remains pivotal.

Prozesse, mit denen das Büro arbeitet. Die „Eindrücke" und „Abdrücke" sollen sich – wie die dazugehörigen Typen – nur allmählich verändern, damit „die Stadt" als Form und Gestalt, als Lebensort und als Zuhause erkennbar bleibt. Die meiste Energie fließt deshalb in die Verbesserung des vorhandenen architektonischen und stadtbaulichen Repertoires. Die Wiederholung und damit die Bestätigung des „Eindrucks" vermittels der morphologischen Reproduktion und Variation der tradierten Typen ist wichtiger als die stete Neuerfindung von Sensationen und Ungesehenem. Das Gemeinsame bleibt schlussendlich bedeutender als das Individuelle.

Nur das behutsame, rationale Abwägen von Vorteilen und Nachteilen, nur eine sensible Abwägung von Interessen lässt die dafür nötigen produktiven und dauerhaften Diskussions- und Prozessergebnisse erwarten. Zu diesen Ergebnissen gehören indes nicht nur akzeptable, ästhetisch wahrnehmbare Formen und Figuren. Dazu gehört auch, dass urbane Veränderungen auf ein menschengemäßes Tempo reduziert und stadtbauliche und architektonische Eingriffe zu größtmöglicher Verträglichkeit gebracht werden. Betrachtet man den eigentlichen Sinn von „Politik" als Sorge um die Zukunft der gemeinsamen Sache, so ist das Handeln von ASTOC Architects and Planners in hohem Maße „politisch", nämlich im Sinne der Gesellschaft für die Zukunft verantwortlich. An dieser Haltung hätte wohl auch Leon Battista Alberti gefallen gefunden.

Anmerkungen

1   Croset, Pierre-Alain (Hg.): *Luigi Snozzi. Progetti e architetture 1957–1984*. Mailand 1984
2   Alberti, Leon Battista: *De re aedificatoria*. V.14 (vor 1452, Erstausgabe 1485, vgl.: Theuer, Max: (Hg.): *Leon Battista Alberti: Zehn Bücher über die Baukunst,*.Wien 1912 (Reprint Darmstadt 1991), S. 262
3   ASTOC Architects and Planners: *2010*. Köln 2010, S. 2
4   Siehe Winkler, Olaf: „ASTOC. Der Prozess ist nicht das Ziel". In: *Der Architekt* 5/6, 2005, S. 66ff.
5   Neppl, Markus: „Bauen in Hafengebieten". In: ASTOC Architects and Planners: *2010*. Köln 2010, S. 5
6   Ebd.
7   Vgl. ASTOC Architects and Planners: *2010*. Köln 2010, S. 10f.
8   Vgl. ASTOC Architects and Planners: *Holzhafen Hamburg*. Köln 2010

9   Vgl. ASTOC Architects and Planners: *Siedlung Buchheimer Weg Köln*. Köln 2010. Dass ASTOC die gesamte Bandbreite des Wohnungsbaus beherrscht, haben die Architekten im Übrigen mit einer Mehrfamilienhaussiedlung im Schweizerischen Zug und mit einer Folge von Stadtvillen in Düsseldorf gezeigt. Siehe ASTOC Architects and Planners: *Wohnen Herti 6 Zug*. Köln 2010 sowie dies.: *Orsoyer Straße Düsseldorf*. Köln 2010
10 Vgl. ASTOC Architects and Planners: *2010*. Köln 2010, S. 30
11 Vgl. ASTOC Architects and Planners: *Friesenplatz Köln*. Köln 2010
12 ASTOC Architects and Planners: *2010*, Köln 2010, S. 12, 13 bzw. 35
13 ASTOC Architects and Planners: *Pumpwerk Köln*. Köln 2010
14 ASTOC Architects and Planners: *2010*. Köln 2010, S. 36
15 Ebd., S. 18f.

Only a careful, rational assessment of advantages and disadvantages, and only a sensible evaluation of interests can lead to productive and durable results of discussions and processes. This should not only result in acceptable and aesthetically tangible forms and figures. It also means that urban changes are brought down to the human scale and that urban planning and architectural interventions harmonize to the greatest extent possible. If the practice of politics is taken to literally describe the concern for common welfare, the work and actions of ASTOC Architects and Planners can be said to be highly political: firmly oriented towards the future to ensure the welfare of the common good, something that Leon Battista Alberti would have approved of.

Notes

1   Croset, Pierre-Alain (ed.): *Luigi Snozzi. Progetti e architetture 1957–1984*. Milan, 1984
2   Alberti, Leon Battista: *De re aedificatoria*. V.14 (before 1452, first edition 1485, see: Theuer, Max: (ed.): *Leon Battista Alberti: Zehn Bücher über die Baukunst*, Vienna 1912 (Reprint Darmstadt 1991), p. 262
3   ASTOC Architects and Planners: *2010*. Cologne 2010, p. 2
4   see Winkler, Olaf: „ASTOC. Der Prozess ist nicht das Ziel", in: *Der Architekt* 5/6, 2005, pp. 66
5   Neppl, Markus: "Bauen in Hafengebieten", in: ASTOC Architects and Planners: *2010*. Cologne 2010, p. 5
6   ibid.
7   see ASTOC Architects and Planners: *2010*. Cologne 2010, p. 10
8   see ASTOC Architects and Planners: *Holzhafen Hamburg*. Cologne 2010
9   see ASTOC Architects and Planners: *Siedlung Buchheimer Weg Köln*. Cologne 2010. ASTOC's proficiency in handling all types of residential building projects is also exemplified by their apartment complex in Zug, Switzerland, and a series of city villas in Düsseldorf. See ASTOC Architects and Planners: *Wohnen Herti 6 Zug*. Cologne 2010, and: *Orsoyer Strasse Düsseldorf*. Cologne 2010
10 see ASTOC Architects and Planners: *2010*. Cologne 2010, p. 30
11 see ASTOC Architects and Planners: *Friesenplatz Köln*. Cologne 2010
12 ASTOC Architects and Planners: *2010*, Cologne 2010, p. 12, 13 and 35
13 ASTOC Architects and Planners: *Pumpwerk Köln*. Cologne 2010
14 ASTOC Architects and Planners: *2010*. Cologne 2010, p. 36
15 ibid., pp. 18

PROJEKTE
PROJECTS

HOLZHAFEN HAMBURG
HOLZHAFEN HAMBURG

BÜROGEBÄUDE OST, HOLZHAFEN, HAMBURG
OFFICE BUILDING "EAST", HOLZHAFEN, HAMBURG

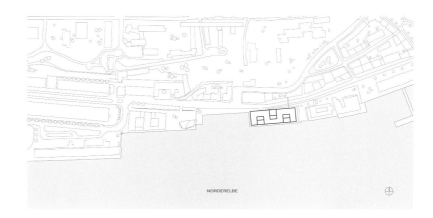

NORDERELBE

Mit dem Bauforum 1985 leitete der damalige Hamburger Ober-baudirektor Egbert Kossak die Revitalisierung des nördlichen Hamburger Elbufers ein. Architekten aus aller Welt entwickelten damals Ideen für den Hafenrand in Hamburg-Altona. Der Struktur-wandel des Hafens ermöglichte die Öffnung der Stadt zur Elbe. Der Holzhafen ist das älteste Hafenbecken in Hamburg und liegt zwischen dem Fährterminal und dem berühmten Hamburger Fischmarkt. Die neuen Wohn- und Bürohäuser, die entlang der Großen Elbstraße gebaut wurden, bieten fantastische Ausblicke auf die Elbe und den Hamburger Hafen. Der in einem internatio-nalen Wettbewerb ausgezeichnete Entwurf für die Bebauung des Holzhafens von ASTOC, Kees Christiaanse und Christian Herbert wurde in der Folge überarbeitet und die Büroflächen zugunsten von Wohnungen reduziert. Am Holzhafen selbst wurde ein durch-gängiger Weg mit öffentlichen Plätzen an der Elbe geschaffen. ASTOC, Kees Christiaanse und Christian Herbert sahen in ihrem Entwurf drei Gebäude vor: Zwei flankierende Bürogebäude mit Backsteinfassaden rahmen dabei einen zwanziggeschossigen glä-sernen Wohnturm. Die drei Gebäude bilden somit eine kontinuier-liche Wasserfront.

Traditionell liegt zwischen der Hamburger Innenstadt und der Elbe ein schmaler Streifen Lagerhäuser, wie in der berühmten Speicher-stadt. Die Speicher haben in der Regel rote Backsteinfassaden. Dieses Motiv greift der Entwurf für den Holzhafen auf.

With the conclusion of the Bauforum in 1985, Hamburg's then sen-ior construction director, Egbert Kossak, ushered in a period of revi-talization of Hamburg's northern Elbe River banks. Architects from around the world were invited to submit new ideas for redevelop-ing Hamburg-Altona's harbor rim. Economic structural change had a direct impact on port activities, offering a unique chance for the city to grow closer to the Elbe River. The Holzhafen is the oldest inner harbor in Hamburg and lies between the ferry terminal and the famous Hamburg fish market. New residential and office build-ings built along the Grosse Elbstrasse offer grand views of the Elbe River and the city's port. The prize-winning design, selected in an international competition and jointly submitted by ASTOC, Kees Christiaanse, and Christian Herbert, was later modified to reduce office space and offer more apartment space. At the Holzhafen itself, a continuous street with public squares by the banks of the Elbe River was laid out. ASTOC, Kees Christiaanse, and Christian Herbert envisaged three new buildings in their design: two office buildings with clinker facades that flank a twenty-story glazed resi-dential tower, making up a continuous waterfront.

Traditionally, there has always been a narrow strip of warehouses between Hamburg's inner city and the Elbe River, as found in the famous Speicherstadt, for example. The warehouses are usually clad in red clinker, a motif that has been incorporated into the de-sign of the new building.

Der städtebauliche Entwurf ist abgeleitet aus dem Wechsel von massiven Lagerhäusern und Freiräumen entlang der Kai-Kante der Elbe. Die beiden Bürogebäude fassen als Ziegelgebäude das kristallin wirkende gläserne Wohngebäude am Hafenbecken. Die Gebäude gehören zu dem unter der Leitung von Senatsbaudirektor Kossak entwickelten Planungsprinzip, das eine „Perlenkette" zwischen Elbhang und Fluss entlang der Hamburger Waterkant vorsah. Die Stadt sollte wieder an das Wasser herangeführt werden.

Das Bürogebäude Ost bietet 16.000 Quadratmeter Bruttogeschossfläche und war das erste fertiggestellte Gebäude des baulichen Trios. Es ist wie ein „Fenster zum Hafen" angelegt und fungiert umgekehrt auch als „Fenster zur Stadt". Das siebenstöckige Bürogebäude mit mäandrierenden Grundrissen vermittelt mit seiner Klinkerfassade und seinen sieben Geschossen zwischen den benachbarten historischen Speicherhäusern und den Neubauten. Drei Lichthöfe sorgen für Transparenz und sichern vielen Arbeitsplätzen einen einmaligen Blick auf das Wasser. Alle drei Höfe sind unterschiedlich gestaltet und erzeugen verschiedene Ausblicke und Lichteinfälle. Der mittlere Hof als Eingangshalle ist größer und repräsentativer als die beiden anderen Höfe, weil er als zentraler Zugang und räumliche Visitenkarte des Hauses dient.

Restaurants und Läden im Erdgeschoss sorgen ebenso wie ein hölzerner Fußweg vor dem Gebäude für mehr urbanes Flair im Quartier am Holzhafen. Das Gebäude zeigt Präsenz, ohne den Blick auf die

The urban planning design allows the massive warehouses to playfully alternate with the adjoining open spaces along the quayside edge of the Elbe River. The two brick office buildings elegantly frame the crystal-like glazed residential tower. The ensemble reflects a planning principle originally developed under the leadership of Senate Building Director Kossak that suggests the design of a "string of pearls" between the Elbe River and its sloping banks along Hamburg's Waterkant. The idea was to reconnect Hamburg with its waterfront again.

Providing 16,000 square meters of gross floor area, the office building "East" was the first of the three buildings to be completed. It was envisioned as "a window on the harbor" while inversely also becoming "a window on the city." The new office building with its meandering floor plan architecturally balances the neighboring historical warehouses and the new buildings with its clinker facade and seven floors. Three atriums ensure transparency while providing the workplaces inside with unique views of the river. All three courtyards are differently designed, creating diverse perspectives and lighting conditions. The central courtyard, envisaged to be the entrance hall, is larger and more prestigious than the two other courtyards, serving as both central access point and as the "spatial visiting card" of the building.

Restaurants and shops, located on the first floor, and a wooden footpath in front of the building produce a lively urban flair in the

Elbe zu versperren. Der skulptural geformte Baukörper verknüpft symbolisch die Stadt mit dem Wasser. Das Gebäude ist so perforiert, dass Blicke von der Stadt durch das Gebäude möglich sind. Für die Fassade, die Unterseiten der brückenartigen Bauteile und die Böden wurde ein einheitlicher Ziegel verwendet. Diese Klinkerflächen sind wie eine „Haut" gestaltet. Das bedeutet, dass sie zwar eine angenehme Haptik, Farbigkeit und Textur bringen, sie wurden jedoch nicht nach Innen- oder Außenfassaden differenziert oder mit besonderen Details akzentuiert: Die Detaillierung ist im Gegenteil betont diskret und unauffällig. Selbst die Attiken und Sohlbänke der Fenster wurden als Fertigteile aus demselben Klinker hergestellt, um eine möglichst homogene und durchgehende Wirkung der Fas-

entire Holzhafen district. The building has an impressive presence without obstructing views of the Elbe River. With its sculptural shape, it symbolically links the city with the water. The building facade is perforated to allow for views of the city from the inside. The clinker that has been used to clad the façade also covers the undersides of the bridge-like building elements and the floors. These brick surfaces are designed to be like a "skin." Pleasantly textured and colored, the inside and outside 'skins' are, however, not different from each other while extensive detailing of the 'skin' has been deliberately dispensed with, making it rather discrete and low-key. Even the attics and window sills have been prefabricated from the same clinker to maximize homogeneity and continuity of

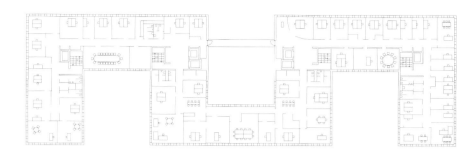

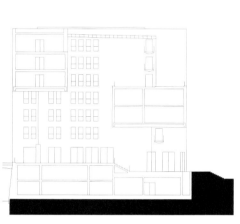

saden zu erzielen. Das gilt auch für die elastischen Seilfassaden, die eine rahmenlose Verglasung der zentralen Eingangshalle tragen. Die Fassaden wirken so, als würden sie tatsächlich nur aus Stein oder Glas bestehen.

Für den Fall einer Sturmflut und eines damit verbundenen Hochwassers, wie es den Holzhafen regelmäßig heimsucht, haben die Planer bei der Gestaltung des Bürohauses vorgesorgt und eine elegante Fußgängerbrücke zu einem Bürohaus desselben Bauherren auf der anderen Seite der Großen Elbstraße am Fuß des Elbhangs gebaut, über die man bei Hochwasser „von oben" an seinen Arbeitsplatz gelangen kann.

the facades. This also applies to the elastic cable-suspended and frameless glazed facade that fronts the central entrance hall. At the same time, the facades as a whole appear as if consisting only of stone and glass.

For the event of a storm surge and a subsequent flood which may regularly occur at the site of the Holzhafen, the planners devised an elegant pedestrian bridge that leads to an office building (belonging to the same client) on the other side of the *Grosse Elbstrasse*, at the foot of the Elbe River slopes, that would provide employees with an alternative route to their place of work "from above."

WOHNHOCHHAUS AM HOLZHAFEN, HAMBURG
HIGH-RISE APARTMENT BUILDING, HOLZHAFEN, HAMBURG

Zwischen den beiden ziegelverkleideten Bürogebäuden steht das Wohnhochhaus als kristalliner, vielkantiger Körper. Aus verschiedenen Blickwinkeln vom Hang und den umgebenden Gebäuden aus schafft es neue Sichtbeziehungen. Das Haus steht auf einem schwarzen Natursteinsockel und teilt sich in den oberen Geschossen durch die Erschließungszone in zwei „Arme" auf. Diese haben die Form eines unregelmäßigen Fünfecks und eines unregelmäßigen Vierecks. Das Gebäude ist so geformt, dass man von jedem Standpunkt aus stets mehrere Gebäudekanten gleichzeitig sieht und so immer verschiedene Fassadenabschnitte in Licht und Schatten stehen. Diese kristalline Erscheinung wird durch eine plane Glasfassade mit außenbündigen Kastenfenstern verstärkt. Der prismatische Körper bietet 9000 Quadratmeter Wohnfläche für 37 exklusive Eigentumswohnungen mit Hafen- und Stadtpanorama. Alle Wohnungen verfügen über große Außenbereiche: tiefe, windgeschützte Balkone, Loggien oder Dachterrassen. Die Wohnungen bieten weite Ausblicke auf die nahe Schiffswende in der Elbe und die Köhlbrandbrücke im Hintergrund. Sie sind zwischen 120 und 360 Quadratmeter groß.

In die exklusiven Apartments gelangt man mit einem der zwei gläsernen Aufzüge, die außen an der Nordseite des Turmes auf- und abfahren und so die Fahrt zur Wohnungstür zu einem visuellen Erlebnis machen. Im unteren Teil des Turmes liegen drei Wohnungen pro Etage, im oberen Bereich zwei. (Ab dem 13. Obergeschoss aufwärts sind zwei Wohnungen zu einer Geschosswohnung zusammengelegt). Die Wohnungen werden nach den Wünschen der Käufer von verschiedenen Innenarchitekten gestaltet. Gemeinsam ist ihnen nur ihr hoher Ausbaustandard. Alle Apartments haben hohe Räume. Die fein gerahmten Doppelfenster werden durch Lüftungsflügel ergänzt. Der Wohnturm teilt sich mit dem benachbarten Bürohaus ein gemeinsames, dreigeschossiges Tiefgaragen-Plateau.

Vor dem beeindruckenden Panorama des Elbhangs zeigt sich das Gebäude mit einem plastisch ausformulierten Baukörper, der weithin sichtbar ist.

Nestling between two brick-clad office buildings, the new high-rise apartment building appears as a crystalline, multisided edifice. Viewed from various angles such as from the slope and the surrounding buildings, it continuously establishes new visual relationships. The building rests on a black natural stone base and is divided into two wings on the upper floors due to its circulation zone. One wing is shaped like an irregular pentagon, and the other, like an irregular rectangle. The building has been designed so that several sides can be seen simultaneously from various positions with the result that light and shadow playfully alternate on different parts of the facade. This crystalline appearance is reinforced by a flat glazed facade with flush-mounted casement windows. The prismatic built volume provides 9,000 square meters of residential space to accommodate 37 exclusive freehold apartments with panoramic views of the port and the city. All apartments come with generous open spaces such as deep, wind-protected balconies, loggias or roof terraces. The apartments, ranging in size from 120 to 360 square meters, offer magnificent views of the ship turning area in the Elbe River and the Köhlbrand Bridge in the background.

Access to the exclusive apartments is by means of one of two glazed elevators that run up and down the north side of the tower, making the ascent to the dwellings a memorable visual experience. The lower part of the tower houses three apartments on each floor, the upper part two. From the thirteenth floor onwards, two apartments are laid out as stacked floor types. Depending on the preferences of buyers, the interiors are individually designed by various interior architects. What all apartments have in common is, however, their high-quality building and interior standards, as well as their high ceilings. The delicately framed double windows are complemented by vent sashes. A three-storied underground garage is common to both the apartment tower and the neighboring office building. The client for all three buildings was the Hamburg-based B&L Group.

With the panoramic slopes of the Elbe as backdrop, the building appears as an elegant, sculptural piece of architecture that is visible from afar.

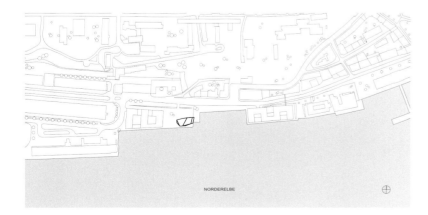

NORDERELBE

BÜROGEBÄUDE WEST, HOLZHAFEN, HAMBURG
OFFICE BUILDING "WEST", HOLZHAFEN, HAMBURG

Die Prinzipien des Bürogebäudes Ost wurden bei dem westlichen Bürohaus am Hamburger Holzhafen adaptiert, variiert und auf ein tieferes und kürzeres Grundstück übertragen. Das Haus hat im Gegensatz zu seinem östlichen Pendant nur zwei statt drei Höfe. Das Bürogebäude soll durch seine homogenen Fassaden und großen Ausschnitte wie „ein Stein mit Löchern" wirken. Wenn große Schiffe auf der Elbe vorbeifahren, stellen sie die Dimension der Gebäude am Holzhafen in den Schatten. Die strenge Lochfassade des östlichen Gebäudes wurde hier modifiziert und das Haus stärker zum Wasser hin ausgerichtet. Eine „sägezahnartig" gefaltete Glasfassade, die um die Gebäudeecken herumgeführt wurde, ermöglicht auch an den Ost- und Westseiten des Gebäudes einen direkten Blick auf die Elbe. Die Grundrisse sind so gestaltet, dass pro Etage bis zu sechs Mieteinheiten mit jeweils mindestens 200 Quadratmetern Fläche eingerichtet werden können. Dabei sind sowohl riegel- als auch L-förmige Mieteinheiten möglich.

Die begehbaren Dachflächen wurden als hölzerne Decks gestaltet. Das Material erinnert an das Hauptumschlagsgut im ehemaligen Holzhafen. Zum umweltfreundlichen Energiekonzept gehört der Einsatz von Erdwärmekollektoren in Kombination mit einer Betonkern-Aktivierung. Die Doppelfassade sorgt für optimalen Schallschutz, ein angenehmes Raumklima und ungetrübte Ausblicke auf den Hafen. Sie gewährleistet darüber hinaus eine natürliche Belüftung der Büros. Die mäanderförmig gegliederten Fassaden schaffen einen Bezug zum benachbarten Bürogebäude Ost. Sämtliche Bürogeschosse sind flexibel aufteilbar.

Das Bürogebäude West am Holzhafen schließt das Konzept der städtebaulichen „Perlenkette" mit einem Baukörper ab, der beweist, dass große Volumen nicht massig wirken müssen, sondern verschiedene räumliche Qualitäten bieten können.

For its "western" counterpart, the principles that had been applied to the office building "East" have been adapted and modified to fit a lower lying and shorter site at Hamburg's Holzhafen. Compared to the eastern building, the western one only has two instead of three courtyards. The idea was that the office building, with its homogenous facades and large openings, should look like a "stone with holes". The big ships passing by on the Elbe River dwarf the buildings at the Holzhafen. The somewhat somber-looking perforated facade of the eastern building was modified for the western one, while also bringing it closer to the water. A saw-toothed and folded glass facade that runs around the corners of the building allows for direct views of the Elbe River even on the eastern and western sides of the building. The floor plans have been designed to accommodate up to six rented units per floor, each at least 200 square meters in size. Both oblong as well as L-shaped rented units have been provided.

The walkable roof surfaces were laid out as decks made of wood, recalling the main trading material of the former Holzhafen. The building's eco-friendly energy concept includes geothermal heat collectors combined with concrete core activation. The double facade ensures optimal soundproofing, a pleasant indoor climate and unobstructed views of the docks, while it also makes possible natural ventilation of the offices. The meandering facades create references to the neighboring eastern office building. All office floors can be flexibly divided. The office building "West" at the Holzhafen elegantly rounds off the urban planning concept of the "string of pearls", exemplifying the fact that large built volumes don't necessarily have to be bulky, but can, on the contrary, offer a wide new range of spatial qualities.

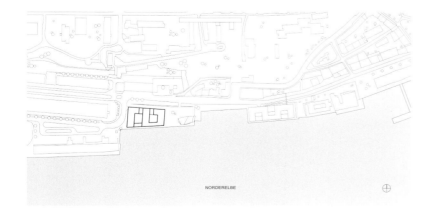

NORDERELBE

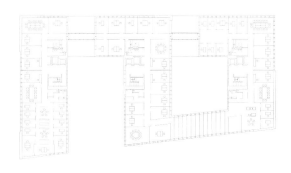

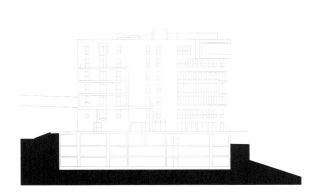

PUMPWERK, KÖLN
PUMPING STATION, COLOGNE

Moos hat die Fähigkeit, Wasser zu filtern. Frisches, sauberes Wasser ist ein kostbares Gut. Die Infrastruktur, die für die Herstellung, Reinigung und Verteilung von Wasser in den großen Städten nötig ist, ist jedoch weitgehend unsichtbar. Da lag es nahe, dass das neue Kölner Pumpwerk am Rhein diesen Prozess mit einer Mooswand im Straßenraum sichtbar macht. Sie verbildlicht die Reinigung des Wassers, die – allerdings mit hohem technischem Aufwand, anders als beim stillen, weichen Moos – Zweck des Gebäudes ist. Hauptaufgabe des Pumpwerks ist die Regenwasserklärung zur Einleitung in den Rhein. Das Gebäude gibt dem unsichtbaren Prozess eine Gestalt. Das Hochwasserpumpwerk ist eines von sieben neu gebauten Pumpwerken, die sich wie eine „Perlenkette" entlang des Rheins gliedern.

Moos ist ein durchaus anspruchsvolles Gewächs, das ständige Feuchtigkeit liebt und direkte Sonne scheut. Entlang des Rheins gedeiht es bevorzugt an den Stellen, an denen Wasserspiegel sin-

Moss can filter water which, when fresh and clean, is a most precious good. The infrastructure required to produce, purify, and distribute water in large cities is, however, mostly hidden from public view. It therefore seemed obvious that the new pumping station in Cologne, located by the banks of the Rhine River, would make this process visible by means of a wall of moss facing the street. It serves to illustrate the basic purification process of water even though the new building houses elaborate filtering technology that is rather different from that of gentle moss-based filtering. The pumping station's main task is to treat rainwater before it is released into the Rhine River. As such, the building reflects this internal process in tangible terms. The storm water pumping station is one of seven new pumping stations that line the Rhine like a "string" of pearls.

A discerning plant, moss favors permanently moist environments and eschews direct sunlight. Along the Rhine River, it mostly

ken und steigen. Mit Hilfe von Moos-Fachkompetenz der Universität Bonn, auch Bryologie genannt, gelang es, kleine Moos-Flächen an der befeuchteten Basaltwand anwachsen zu lassen. Die horizontalen Fugen entlang der neun Meter hohen und 40 Meter langen Wand geben dem Moos Gelegenheit Wurzeln zu schlagen, und der Fassadengestaltung eine Prise „Jazz". An den Fugen, die mit gereinigtem Regenwasser berieselt werden, entsteht der grüne Pelz zuerst. Industrielles Streckmetall wurde auf den flussabgewandten Fassaden verwendet und Mendiger Basalt auf der Seite zum Rhein. Die Fassadengestaltung spiegelt damit auch die beiden städtebaulichen Seiten wider: Die Umgebung des Grundstücks an der St.-Leonardus-Straße ist auf der einen Seite von anspruchslosen Industrie- und Gewerbegebäuden geprägt – auf der anderen lockt die Auenlandschaft des Rheinufers. Hier wurde in einem Gewerbegebiet eine ansehnliche Fassade gebaut. Basalt wurde gewählt, weil auch die Mauern entlang der Flusspromenade traditionell aus

thrives in areas where water levels alternately rise and fall. Utilizing Bonn University's professional expertise on moss, the study of which is collectively known as bryology, it became possible to plant small patches of moss on a moistened basalt wall. The horizontal gaps along the nine meter high and forty meter long wall allow the moss to strike roots, lending the facade a charming jazzy note. It is at these gaps, sprinkled with rain water, that the "green coat" grows first. Industrial expanded metal was used on those facades that face away from the river, while Mendig basalt was used on the side facing it. The facade design itself reflects both urban development sides of the site: the surroundings of the plot at St.-Leonardus-Strasse are characterized on the one side by rather nondescript industrial and commercial buildings, and on the other by the enticing meadow landscape of the Rhine River banks. Here, in this conventional-looking commercial area, a handsome facade has been built. Basalt was chosen since the walls along the river

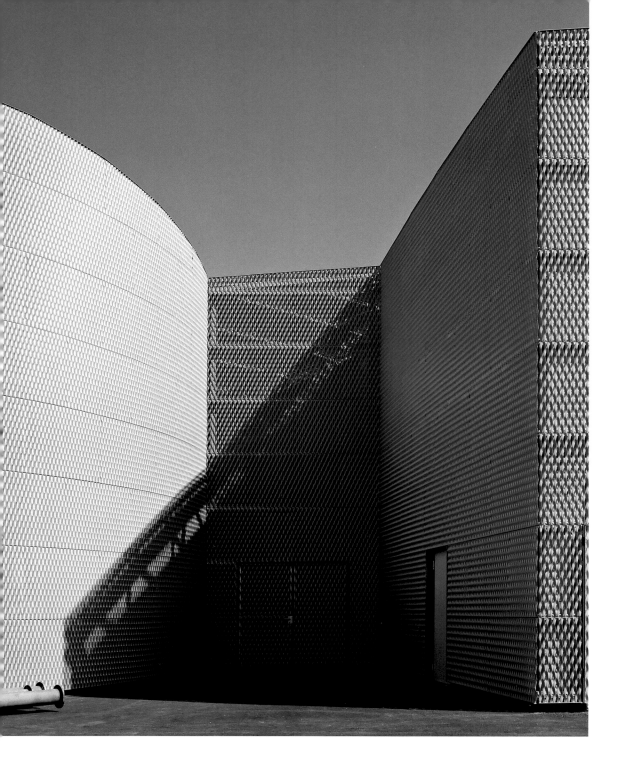

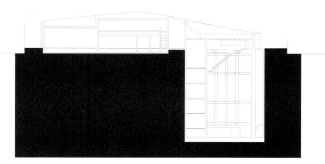

diesem dunklen Stein hergestellt werden. Das Streckmetall der rückseitigen Anlage bildet eine Fassade als leichte Hülle aus, um die verschiedenen Geräte, denen die Anlage Platz bietet, ohne Witterungsschutz zu fassen.

Der Entwurf fügt die technischen Bauteile zu einem Volumen und ordnet sie unter einer Gebäudehülle an. Der überwiegende Anteil liegt unter der Erde. Die Geometrie des Gebäudes ist durchaus komplex: Die geschwungene Basaltwand beispielsweise ist in beide Richtungen gekrümmt. Vor dem Gebäude entstand so ein kleiner öffentlicher Platz, hinter dem Gebäude liegt ein Regenklärbecken. Neben einigen technischen Funktionen, wie zum Beispiel Generatoren und Transformatoren, bietet das straßenbegleitende Gebäude vor allem den Zugang zu den fünf Untergeschossen, in denen sich die großen Pumpen und „Schieber" befinden, die die Stadt vor Hochwasser schützen.

Das Kölner Pumpwerk zeigt die Regenwasserreinigung als Teil des ökologischen Prozesses. Bei Wasserverschmutzung zeigen Moose organische und chemische Belastung an, Gewässerversauerung und Schwermetallbelastung – ein besseres architektonisch einsetzbares Symbol für die Qualität des Kölner Wassers, das in Form und Lage im Rheinraum verankert ist, gibt es also nicht.

promenade have traditionally been constructed out of this dark stone. The expanded metal used on the rear facility has a facade shaped like a light envelope, encasing the different types of equipment inside, and dispensing with a weather shield.

The design brings together all the technical elements into one built volume, arranging them in a single building envelope of which the larger part lies underground. The building's geometry is rather complex: the meandering basalt wall, for example, is doubly curved, making space for a small public square. A rainwater sedimentation basin lies behind the building. Apart from housing technical equipment such as generators and transformers, the street-facing building provides access to the five basement levels which accommodate the large pumps and "slides" that protect the city from floods. The pumping station in Cologne appropriately reflects the process of ecological rainwater purification. Moss plants are able to indicate organic and chemical pollution, acidification, and heavy-metal contamination in water. The building is a unique and architecturally fitting symbol for the quality of Cologne's water, reflecting the Rhine region in its aesthetics and site-specific planning.

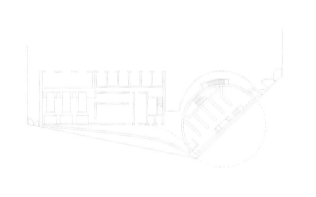

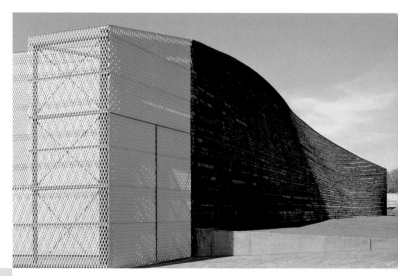

WOHNEN ORSOYER STRASSE, DÜSSELDORF
HOUSING ON ORSOYER STRASSE, DÜSSELDORF

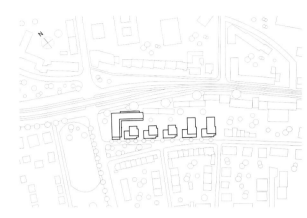

Dass es neben spießiger Reihenhausbauweise, ausufernden Einfamilienhaussiedlungen und sturen Blockrandbebauungen im zeitgenössischen Städtebau noch einen dritten Weg gibt, beweist eindrücklich die Wohnbebauung an der Orsoyer Straße im Norden von Düsseldorf unweit des Rheins. Diese schafft mit sechs großen und kompakten, winkelförmigen Stadtvillen und einem das Grundstück schließenden, ebenfalls winkelförmigen Kopfbau urbane Dichte mit differenzierten und großzügigen Freiräumen. Der formal sehr zurückhaltende Wohnkomplex ist das gelungene Ergebnis eines dialogischen Workshopverfahrens mit Bürgerbeteiligung am „runden Tisch".

Möglich wurde der Neubau durch den Abzug der britischen Truppen aus Nordrhein-Westfalen nach der deutschen Wiedervereinigung, denn die Streitkräfte hatten auf dem Grundstück ihre Offizierswohnungen untergebracht. Die herrlichen alten Platanen am Reeser Platz konnten erhalten werden und verleihen der Straße und dem Wohnumfeld ihren Charme.

Die zweigeschossigen großen und städtischen Reihenhäuser auf der einen Straßenseite sollten von den höheren neuen Nachbarn mit vier und sechs Etagen auf der anderen Seite optisch nicht miniaturisiert werden. Der Entwurf löst den gordischen Knoten im Städtebau und bedient sich einiger einfacher, aber raffinierter Maßnahmen: Um sich in die bestehenden Maßstäbe einzufügen, vermittelt der Bau zwischen einer viergeschossigen Bebauung an der rückwärtigen Kaiserswerther Straße und der zweigeschossigen Bebauung an der Orsoyer Straße, indem die Baumasse in straßenbegleitende und im Volumen gestaffelte Einzelhäuser aufgelöst wird. Das

The housing development at Orsoyer Strasse, close to the Rhine River in the north of Düsseldorf, wonderfully shows that there is more to contemporary urban planning than narrow-minded row-type housing, burgeoning detached housing estates and stubborn perimeter block developments. Its six large but compact and angular city villas as well as another angular front-side building, create a unique urban density with diverse and generous open spaces. The low-key and serene housing complex is the successful result of a dialogic workshop that allowed citizens to participate in a "round table" setting.

Following German re-unification, it was the withdrawal of British troops from North-Rhine Westphalia that made the new buildings possible as the old military officers' apartments on the site became obsolete. The impressive old sycamore trees at Reeser Square have been preserved and lend the street and the surroundings of the housing complex a distinctive charm.

The large two-storied urban row houses on one side of the street have been saved from being dwarfed by their higher and newer neighbors having four or six floors on the other side of the street. The design undoes the Gordian knot in urban planning, employing some simple but refined measures: to fit into existing scales, the building complex architecturally mediates between a four-story building complex on Kaiserswerther Strasse in the rear and the two-story building development at Orsoyer Strasse, by dividing the entire building mass into street-lining and internally stacked, individual buildings. This not only leads to more friendly neighbors, but also provides improved natural lighting and ventilation, creating a larger

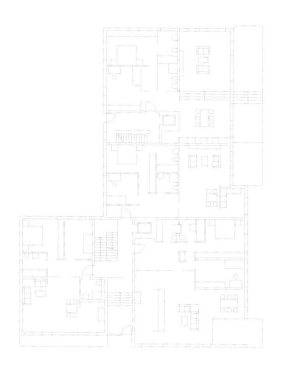
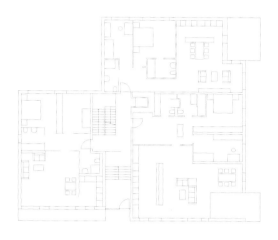

führt nicht nur zu einem freundlicheren Nachbarn, sondern bietet auch den Vorteil der besseren natürlichen Belichtung und Belüftung und schafft mehr Fassadenfläche, die für französische Fenster und große Balkone genutzt wird. Räumliche Qualität und hohe Dichte scheinen sich plötzlich nicht mehr auszuschließen, sondern sogar im Gegenteil einander zu befördern. ASTOC hatte sich mit seinem Konzept in einem Wettbewerb durchgesetzt und das Projekt vom städtebaulichen Entwurf über die Bebauungsplanung bis zu den kleinsten architektonischen Details gestalten können – eine gute Grundlage für die ungewöhnlich hohe und konsistente Qualität der Wohnanlage. Bauherr war die Bayerische Hausbau aus München.

Um einen klar formulierten Innenhof entstanden weiße Stadtvillen mit Gartenanteil und großen Loggien. Um Rücksicht auf den Maßstab der Nachbarbebauung zu nehmen, haben die weiß verputzten Kuben ebenfalls eine Traufhöhe von nur zwei Etagen. Die Gebäudeecken sind geöffnet, um Raum für Loggien zu bieten und den Baukörpern zusätzliche Leichtigkeit zu geben. Die oberen beiden Stockwerke sind zurückgestaffelt und haben einen Austritt auf

facade surface used for French windows and generous balconies. Spatial quality and high density suddenly don't seem to exclude one another anymore, but on the contrary, appear to support each other. ASTOC was able to win the competition with their unique concept, permitting the firm to design everything from the urban plan to the development plan and to the smallest architectural details. This provided ideal conditions for achieving the unusually high and consistent quality of the housing complex's design. The client was the Bayerische Hausbau from Munich.

A crisply designed courtyard groups a series of white city villas with gardens and generous loggias around it. Taking into consideration the neighboring buildings, the white plastered cubes also have an eaves height of only two floors. Building corners have been left free to leave space for loggias and to give the buildings additional lightness. The two upper floors are stacked back and lead on to large roof gardens. On the narrowest part of the plot there are square townhouses and, wherever the shape of the site permits, larger townhouses with a greater depth.

große Dachgärten. An der schmalsten Stelle des Grundstücks gibt es quadratische und wo es die Form des Grundstücks zulässt, auch tiefere Stadthäuser.

Ebenso wichtig wie die Gestaltung der Häuser und der Wohnungen ist die Ausformulierung der Freiflächen. Sie sind sorgfältig abgestuft und führen vom öffentlichen über einen halböffentlichen Bereich zu den privaten Außenräumen der Bewohner. Eine niedrige Natursteinmauer grenzt die Gärten von der Straße ab und greift dieses in der Nachbarschaft verwendete Material auf. Der Verlust an Grünfläche und die Versiegelung wird durch intensiv begrünte Dachgärten und extensiv begrünte Flachdächer kompensiert, die zugleich das Stadtklima in dem dicht bebauten Stadtteil verbessern.

Die Grundrisse sind variabel und vielfältig gestaltet, auch um eine soziale Mischung der Anwohnerstruktur in der Straße zu befördern. Die Wohnungsgrößen reichen dabei von 65 bis 200 Quadratmeter. Das elegante gestalterische Understatement, das die Baukörper prägt, findet sich auch im Inneren der Gebäude wieder, die Häuser wirken zugleich wohnlich und edel.

The design of the open spaces was as important as that of the buildings and apartments. The open spaces are carefully graded and lead from a public space via a semi-public space to the private open spaces of the residents. A low natural stone wall shields the gardens from the street, while utilizing a material that has characteristically shaped the neighborhood. The loss of green spaces and the sealing of the soil are compensated by green roofs, including extensive flat green roofs that also serve to improve the city climate in this densely packed urban district.

The ground plans have been designed to be flexible and versatile, encouraging a good social mix of the resident population in the street. Apartments range from 65 to 200 square meters in size. Inside, the elegantly understated quality of the buildings is also clearly discernible, appearing both homely and noble.

BAHNSTATIONEN SOLINGEN MITTE UND GRÜNEWALD
RAILROAD STATIONS SOLINGEN MITTE AND GRÜNEWALD

Die Stadt Solingen ist vor allem für die Herstellung von Scheren und Messern bekannt. Der Aufschwung der Solinger Metallwaren-Betriebe begann schon 1794 mit der Verleihung von Scherenmacher-Privilegien. Nur 17 Jahre später ließ Johann Abraham Gottlieb Fries in Solingen die Herstellung von Tiegelgussstahl patentieren.

Im Zuge der Industrialisierung schnell gewachsen, ist die Stadt Solingen heute ein Konglomerat aus kleineren, miteinander verschmolzenen Siedlungskernen. Fünf Städte wurden 1929 zur Großstadt Solingen vereinigt. Zwischen diesen Zentren wurden die unterschiedlichsten Verkehrswege gesponnen: Bis heute sind die sechs Linien der Oberleitungsbusse ein markantes Charakteristikum der Stadt geblieben und Solingen hat mit einer speziellen, nicht mehr betriebenen „Oberleitungsbus-Drehscheibe" im Stadtteil Burg und der Müngstener Brücke, der höchsten Eisenbahnbrücke Deutschlands, zwei einzigartige historische Verkehrsbauwerke zu bieten. Anschluss an das Eisenbahnnetz bekam Solingen 1867 und nur 20 Jahre später wurde zusätzlich die wegen ihrer kurvenreichen Trassierung durch das Bergische Land „Korkenzieherbahn" genannte Linie eröffnet. 1897 fuhr in Solingen erstmals eine elektrische Straßenbahn, die erst 1952 durch einen Oberleitungsbus ersetzt wurde.

The city of Solingen is known for its manufacture of scissors and knives. The growth of the metal goods industry in Solingen already began in 1794 when scissor-making rights and privileges were granted. Only seventeen years later, Johann Abraham Gottlieb Fries patented the manufacture of crucible steel in Solingen.

Having experienced rapid growth during industrialization, the city of Solingen today is a conglomerate of small interconnected settlement cores. Five cities were joined in 1929 to make up the larger city of Solingen. Many different transport routes were built between these centers. Till today, the six trolleybus lines have remained a characteristic feature of the city. Solingen can boast of two unique historical traffic infrastructure monuments: the now defunct trolleybus hub in the district of Burg, and the Müngstener Bridge which is Germany's highest railroad bridge. The city was connected to the railroad network in 1867, and only twenty years later, the so-called "corkscrew railroad," appropriately named on account of its winding tracks running through the hilly Bergische Land, was also inaugurated. The first electric tram began to operate in Solingen in 1897, only replaced in 1952 by a trolleybus service.

In a city like Solingen that has brought together various cities through municipal territorial reform and the extension of the urban

Bahnstation Solingen Grünewald Railroad Station Solingen Grünewald 2007   51,163811° 7,079660°

In einer – durch kommunale Gebietsreform und Erweiterung des Stadtgebietes – zusammengewachsenen Stadt wie Solingen kann die Gestaltung der Bauten für die städtischen Verkehrsmittel bei der urbanen Identitätsstiftung eine entscheidende Rolle spielen. Darauf zielt auch der Entwurf zweier Haltepunkte von ASTOC ab. Denn seit im Zuge der „Regionale 2006" der Hauptbahnhof Solingen stillgelegt und zum „Forum für Produktdesign" umfunktioniert wurde, wird der Bahnhof Solingen-Ohligs „Hauptbahnhof" genannt. Ersetzt wurde der frühere Hauptbahnhof durch die neuen Haltepunkte Solingen-Grünewald und Solingen-Mitte. Sie verbinden das O-Busnetz mit dem S-Bahnnetz Rhein-Ruhr.

Die Bus- und Bahnstation Grünewald wurde im Zuge dieser Umstrukturierungen zu einem „Tor zur Stadt" aufgewertet. Wie auch bei der anderen Station dient ihr markantes Metalldach als Orientierungspunkt innerhalb der Stadt. Die Umsteigestation liegt direkt neben den Zwillingswerken, dem vielleicht berühmtesten Arbeitgeber der Stadt, und der neue Bahnhof dient in beide Richtungen als städtisches Merkzeichen.

Die organische Grundform des Bahnhofs Mitte ist ganz aus den umgebenden Verkehrsströmen abgeleitet. Die Station liegt zwischen zwei Brücken über einer Bahntrasse und bietet entlang von drei tangentialen Verkehrswegen allen Umsteigern eine trockene, fußläufige Verbindung.

Für die Architekten lag es nahe, in einer von der Metallverarbeitung geprägten Stadt auch für die beiden Stationen Metall zu verwenden. Jegliche Schwere ist den Bauten dennoch fremd: Die leichten

area, the design of public transport buildings can play a decisive role for the process of defining an urban identity. This is also what ASTOC's design for two railroad stations aims to exemplify. Ever since Solingen's central station was shut down following the "Regionale 2006" event, transforming it into the "Forum for Product Design", the Solingen-Ohligs station was temporarily called the new "central station." The former central station has now been replaced by the new stops at Solingen-Grünewald and Solingen-Mitte. They link the trolleybus network with the commuter train network Rhein-Ruhr.

The bus and railroad station Grünewald has become the new gateway to the city. As in the other station, its distinctive metal roof serves as a landmark within the city. The connecting station lies directly adjacent to the premises of the Zwilling company, arguably Solingen's most famous employer. The new station serves as an urban landmark in both directions.

The organic shape of the station at Mitte is derived entirely from the surrounding traffic flows. It lies nestled between two bridges, hovering above a railroad track, providing a weather-protected walkway for transit passengers along three tangential traffic routes.

For the architects, it appeared logical to use metal as the primary material for the two stations in a city long-shaped by the metal processing industry. Still, the buildings don't appear weighty. The light expanded metal hoods are a distinctive feature and help to define and upgrade the surrounding public space. In direct sunlight, their surfaces create charming reflexes and reflections on the sidewalk.

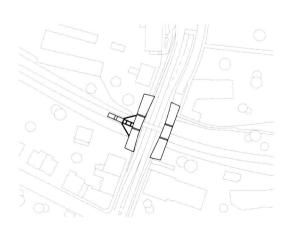

Streckmetallhauben dienen als Imageträger und helfen dabei, den öffentlichen Raum in ihrem Umfeld zu definieren und aufzuwerten. Bei direktem Sonnenlicht werfen ihre Oberflächen reizvolle Reflexe auf das Trottoir. Beide Stationen verbinden das Straßenniveau mit einer tieferliegenden Ebene und bieten einfach zu findende, intuitive Wegeverbindungen. Eine prägnante Gestalt, einfache Benutzbarkeit und hohe Funktionalität waren den Planern gleich wichtig. Schließlich ist die Ausformung der städtischen Infrastruktur eine der wichtigsten Möglichkeiten zur gestalterischen Intervention im Stadtraum und hilft dabei, den ÖPNV attraktiver zu machen.

Both stations link the street level with a lower-lying level, providing easily usable and recognizable route connections. A characteristic shape, convenient usability and a high degree of functionality were equally important for the planners. Finally, the design of urban infrastructure represents one of the most significant opportunities for design-based interventions in the city, helping to make public transport networks even more attractive.

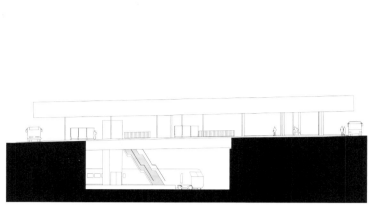

LEBENSMITTELMARKT, KÖLN
FOOD MARKET, COLOGNE

Die typischen ALDI-Supermärkte prägen die Stadtränder und Gewerbegebiete aller deutschen Städte. Mit ihren flachen Satteldächern versuchen sie, ein wenig Biederkeit in die utilitaristischen Umgebungen zu bringen. Mehr als 4000 dieser Filialen gibt es allein in Deutschland. Im Kölner Norden wurde jedoch eine Niederlassung von Deutschlands beliebtestem Billig-Lebensmittelhändler gebaut, die zeigt, dass es auch anders geht: Auch wenn das Raumprogramm in allen ALDI-Supermärkten standardisiert ist, bot doch die Baukörper- und Fassadengestaltung eine seltene Möglichkeit, einem alltäglichen Discount-Markt ein architektonisches Konzept zu verpassen, das langfristig nutzbar ist, Aufmerksamkeit schafft und dennoch in die Corporate Identity passt: Die lichte Raumhöhe des Marktes beispielsweise geht deutlich über die Mindestanforderungen hinaus und macht so eine spätere Umnutzung leichter. Bauherr des Marktes war nämlich nicht die namensgebende Kette, sondern

The ALDI supermarkets are a ubiquitous sight on the outskirts and in the commercial districts of all German cities. With their brown clinker facades and saddle roofs, they look conventional enough to blend into their utilitarian surroundings. There are more than 4,000 ALDI outlets in Germany alone. A new outlet of the country's most popular discount grocer has been built in the north of Cologne, exemplifying an innovative approach. In spite of the fact that space allocation plans are standardized for all ALDI supermarkets, the building and facade design of the new building offered the rare opportunity to apply a long-term architectural concept to this building typology and to draw public attention while still fitting into the client's corporate identity. Take, for instance, the new supermarket's clearance height: it lies well above the minimum requirement, making it easier to convert the space for other future uses. What may come as a surprise is the fact that the client was not the supermar-

eine Versicherung, die die Flächen an ALDI vermietet. Nach Ablauf eines Mietvertrags soll das Gebäude auch für andere Nutzungen geeignet sein und wurde entsprechend auf seine mögliche Nachnutzung hin geplant. Die Architekten verstanden das Gebäude dennoch als Gebrauchs- und nicht als Designobjekt. Das Schachbrettmuster halbiert die Fassadenflächen optisch. Architektonisch ist die Gestaltung der „Box" authentischer und hat mit ihrem einfachen Muster aus dunklen, anthrazitfarbenen und silbrig-hellen Wellblechelementen in unterschiedlichen Ebenen eine Gestaltung bekommen, die dem Körper seine Wucht nimmt. Das Gebäude liegt direkt an einer Bahnlinie und wird deswegen von vielen Vorbeifahrenden nur für den Bruchteil einer Sekunde – als Farbwechsel von hell zu dunkel – wahrgenommen.

ket chain brand itself, but an insurance company that rents out the space to ALDI. Following a tenancy agreement's expiry, the building can, for example, be used for other purposes, and was consciously designed to incorporate this option. At the same time, the architects emphasized the building's utilitarian character, perceiving it not simply as a "design" object. The checkerboard pattern visually divides the facade surfaces in half. Architecturally, the design of the "box" has a raw, authentic quality to it, while its simple patterns, consisting of dark, anthracite-colored and light silver-colored corrugated sheets found on different levels takes the edge off the building. The building lies directly adjacent to a railroad track, allowing people riding by to suddenly experience an instantaneous and dramatic change of color from light to dark as they pass the building.

NEUE DÜSSELDORFER STADTQUARTIERE
NEW URBAN QUARTERS IN DÜSSELDORF

Zu sehen, wie ein gelungener städtebaulicher Entwurf zu einer ebenso gelungenen Architektur führt, ist für Planer, die beide Ebenen bearbeiten, ein Traum. Denn wenn die städtebaulichen Entscheidungen richtig und nachhaltig getroffen wurden, braucht die Architektur nur noch wenig zu ihrem Erfolg. Die „Neuen Düsseldorfer Stadtquartiere", kurz NDS, entstehen nach dem Entwurf von ASTOC. Obwohl Düsseldorf eine wirtschaftlich prosperierende Stadt ist, hat sie, vom eiligen Wiederaufbau nach dem Zweiten Weltkrieg geprägt, aufgrund des eng gefassten Stadtgebiets fast keine attraktiven Wohnquartiere zu bieten. Die Auflassung des ehemaligen Güterbahnhofs im Stadtteil Derendorf bot eine riesige Chance. Zunächst war das Bahngelände jedoch nicht mehr als eine Brache mitten im nördlichen Innenstadtgebiet. Die Vorstellungen der Firma Interboden als Bauherr haben das Areal stark geprägt.

35 Hektar Fläche in bester Lage sollten in ein dichtes Stadtviertel verwandelt werden, neben dem Medienhafen das größte und urbanste städtebauliche Entwicklungsprojekt der Landeshauptstadt. Die hohe Dichte wurde durch die Anlage von großen Grünflächen und eines Erdwalls ausgeglichen, der zudem die neuen Quartiere vor dem Lärm der vorbeifahrenden Züge auf den verbliebenen aktiven Strecken schützt.

Der „2. Grüne Ring" ist Teil einer städtischen Gesamtstrategie und soll die erhöhte urbane Dichte in Teilen der Stadt kompensieren. Während der Gartenarchitekt Maximilian Friedrich Weyhe den „1. Grünen Ring" vom Hofgarten über die Königsallee, den Spee'schen Graben und den Schwanenspiegel bis hin zum Rhein entwarf, entsteht nun seit 2004 der „2. Grüne Ring". Er beginnt am Rheinpark und erstreckt sich über den Hofgarten durch das Gelände des ehemaligen Güterbahnhofs, den Schlachthof, das Rheinmetall-Areal und über den Arnold- und den Golzheimer Platz zum Rheinpark.

Wie ein roter Faden durchzieht ein Stadtgarten dieses neue Stadtviertel mit der Stadtgartenallee als einer breiten, von Baumreihen gesäumten Wegachse.

Der städtebauliche Entwurf orientiert sich an den benachbarten Gründerzeitvierteln. ASTOC hatte sich damit bei einem Wettbe-

Witnessing how a successful urban planning design can lead to equally successful architecture is a dream for planners used to working on both these levels. For when urban planning decisions reflect holistic and sustainable approaches, good architecture follows almost naturally. The New Urban Quarters in Düsseldorf ("Neue Düsseldorfer Stadtquartiere," or NDS for short) are being designed by ASTOC. Although Düsseldorf is a prosperous city, hasty post-war reconstruction during the nineteen-fifties and the city's high urban density led to a dearth of attractive housing quarters. The shutdown of the former goods station in the district of Derendorf offered an exciting new opportunity. Initially, the railway area was not much more than fallow land in the midst of the inner city's northern part. Ideas that the client, the company Interboden, contributed to the project, have strongly shaped the site. The task was to convert thirty-five hectares of prime land into a dense urban district, representing the largest and most urban development project of the state capital together with the Medienhafen project. The high densities were balanced by large green areas and an earth wall which also protects the new quarters from the noise of passing trains on the railway lines that were retained.

The "Second Green Ring" is part of a comprehensive urban planning strategy, having the task of offsetting the increased urban density in parts of the city. While the landscape gardener Maximilian Friedrich Weyhe designed the "First Green Ring" leading from the Hofgarten via the Königsallee, the Spee'schen Graben, and the Schwanenspiegel up to the Rhine River, the "Second Green Ring" is being realized since 2004. It starts at the Rheinpark, passes by the Hofgarten, crosses the site of the former goods station as well as the Schlachthof, the Rheinmetall complex and Arnold and Golzheimer Squares, finally meeting the Rheinpark again. The city garden is like a thread that runs through this new urban district, with the Stadtgartenallee functioning as a broad, tree-lined movement axis.

The urban plan is guided by the design of the neighboring quarters dating from the Wilhelminian period. ASTOC won the urban plan-

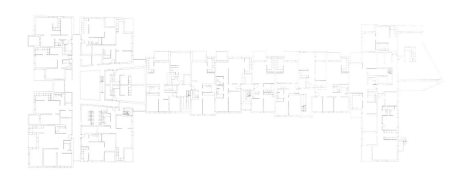

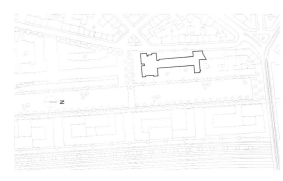

werb im Jahr 2000 durchgesetzt. Das Quartier wurde in der Folge in unterschiedliche Baufelder aufgeteilt: Das 4500 Quadratmeter große „Baufeld 0" ergänzt die bestehende Bebauung entlang der Schinkelstraße und bildet zusammen mit dem „Baufeld 1" den Zugang zu einem neuen Stadtgarten. ASTOC durfte mit der architektonischen Planung des „Baufelds 0" selbst überprüfen, wie sich die städtebaulichen Überlegungen in der gebauten Realität beweisen.

Über einer gemeinsamen Tiefgarage wurden fünf unterschiedliche Wohnhäuser mit insgesamt 129 frei finanzierten Mietwohnungen gebaut. Die lange, schlanke Form der Bahnanlagen wurde beibehalten und tiefe Zeilenbauten ohne Hof vorgeschlagen. Jedes Haus hat seine eigene Adresse und einen eigenen architektonischen Ausdruck: Die Fassade in braunrotem Klinker beispielsweise hebt sich deutlich von ihrem weiß verputzten Pendant ab.

Das Treppenhaus des Kopfbaus – in dem sich allein 63 der insgesamt 129 Wohnungen befinden – erschließt bis zu zehn Wohnungen pro Etage. Es bot somit die Gelegenheit, aus dieser ungewünschten Situation einen großzügigen und durch Oberlicht mit Tageslicht verwöhnten, kommunikativen Innenraum zu machen.

Die Architektur zeichnet sich durch Maßstäblichkeit, Individualität und Flexibilität aus. Das Ziel war ein hohes Maß an Kleinteiligkeit. Neben klassischen Grundrissen wurden Wohnungen mit Dachterrassen und Patiohöfen, Maisonettewohnungen und Lofts realisiert. Die Tiefgarage ragt über das Straßenniveau, sodass ein Hochparterre entsteht. Das schafft nicht nur visuelle Privatsphäre und natürlich belichtete und belüftete Tiefgeschosse, sondern bietet auch Raum für erhöhte Mietergärten, die – nur von Gabionen getrennt – in den

ning competition in 2000. During the execution of the project, the quarter was divided into different building sectors: the 4,500 square meter large "Building Sector 0" complements the existing building stock along Schinkelstrasse, forming the entrance to a new city garden together with "Building Sector 1." With their architectural planning of "Building Sector 0," ASTOC were able to gauge how their urban planning concepts functioned in real space.

Five different apartment buildings with a total of 129 free-financed rented apartments were built on top of a shared underground garage. The long, slender shape of the station premises was retained and deep row-type buildings without courtyards were proposed. Every building has its own address and its own architectural expression: the puce-colored clinker facade, for example, starkly contrasts with its white plastered counterpart.

The staircase of the front building which alone houses as many as 63 of all 129 apartments, provides access to up to ten apartments on each floor, providing the opportunity to convert this rather unwanted spatial situation into one generously lit by daylight from a skylight and with a communicative interior.

The architecture is shaped by human scales, and a sense of individuality and flexibility. The goal was to achieve a high degree of small-scale segmentation. Apart from having classic ground plans, the apartments were furnished with roof terraces and patios, while some were built as duplex types and lofts. The underground garage deliberately sticks out slightly above street level, facilitating the inclusion of a mezzanine floor. This not only provides visual privacy and naturally lit and ventilated basement levels but also cre-

vom Büro Lützow 7 aus Berlin gestalteten benachbarten Park überges.

So entstehen auf dem ehemaligen Güterbahnhof in Derendorf neue Stadtquartiere, die Wohnen, Arbeiten und Leben im Herzen Düsseldorfs ermöglichen. Die gute Infrastruktur, die zentrale Lage und die Anbindung an das öffentliche Verkehrsnetz machen sie ebenso zum begehrten Wohn- und Bürostandort wie die Einbindung in den neuen „Grünen Ring" der Stadt.

ates space for raised tenant gardens that are only a few gabions away from the neighboring park designed by the Berlin-based firm Lützow 7.

In this way, new urban quarters are emerging at the site of the former goods station in Derendorf, enabling novel ways of living and working in the heart of Düsseldorf. Excellent infrastructure, a central location, convenient public transport access, and last but not least, the new urban "green ring" have led to the quarters becoming a much sought-after residential and office location within the city.

SIEDLUNG BUCHHEIMER WEG, KÖLN
HOUSING COMPLEX BUCHHEIMER WEG, COLOGNE

Jede deutsche Stadt hat mehr als eine von ihnen: leicht angestaubte Siedlungen aus den 1950er Jahren in Zeilenbauweise, die schon zu ihrer Bauzeit nicht viel mehr boten als günstigen Wohnraum und weitläufige, unstrukturierte Freiflächen ohne Schnörkel.

Die Zeilenbauweise, wie von den Protagonisten der Moderne propagiert, mag ökonomische Vorteile gehabt haben, städtebaulich zeigten sich ihre Schwächen jedoch unmittelbar: Sie schafft weder lesbare Straßen- noch Grünräume und bildet keine wiedererkennbaren Adressen.

Die Siedlung am Buchheimer Weg im Stadtteil Ostheim von Köln war dafür ein Beispiel. Jetzt, zwei Generationen nach dem Bau, müssen viele dieser Siedlungen technisch erneuert werden und die Gelegenheit ist günstig, ihr Konzept zeitgemäß zu überdenken. Das Ziel ist dabei, die günstige Bauweise für niedrige Einkommensgruppen zu erhalten und dennoch sowohl städtebaulich/freiräumlich als auch architektonisch und innenräumlich neue Qualitäten zu gewinnen. Bauherr ist die Kölner GAG, eine große gemeinnützige Wohnungsbaugesellschaft mit einem Bestand von mehr als 40.000 Wohnungen.

Der Entwurf für den Neubau der Siedlung beweist, dass die Vorteile des Zeilenbaus wie gute Belichtung, Belüftung und Orientierung erhalten bleiben, und dennoch überzeugende Stadträume geschaffen werden können. Die Auseinandersetzung mit dem Siedlungsbau-Erbe der 1950er und 1960er Jahre ist plötzlich hochaktuell geworden und der Entwurf für die Siedlung am Buchheimer Weg bezieht seine größere Bedeutung aus der Tatsache, dass das Projekt durchaus als Modell für andere Siedlungen dieser Art dienen kann – in Köln und anderswo. Denn es bietet bessere räumliche Qualitäten

Every German city has them: dusty old housing complexes dating from the nineteen-fifties that were erected in ribbons which already then were not able to offer much more than cheap housing space and rambling, yet unstructured open spaces without much ado.

Ribbon development, as had been propagated by the protagonists of modernity, may have had its economic benefits, but in urban development terms, its weaknesses became apparent rather quickly: it neither creates legible streets and green spaces nor does it allow for recognizable addresses.

The housing complex at Buchheimer Weg in the urban district of Ostheim in Cologne is a good example for this. Today, two generations after its construction, there are many other old housing complexes that need to be technically renovated. This presents a good opportunity to rethink their concepts to make them suitable for contemporary times and contexts. In doing so, the goal is to retain existing cost-effective structures for low-income groups while creating new qualities in terms of urban planning, open spaces, the architecture and interior design. The client, GAG of Cologne, is a large non-profit building society with a stock of more than 40,000 apartments.

The design for the new housing complex proves that the benefits provided by ribbon development, such as good lighting, ventilation, and orientation, can be retained while simultaneously creating new high-value urban spaces. The debate on the future of the housing complex heritage of the nineteen-fifties and sixties has suddenly become very current today. The design for the housing complex at Buchheimer Weg is significant in that it aspires to serve as a model for other complexes of its kind, both in Cologne and elsewhere. This may not be surprising, as it offers much-improved spatial quali-

und abgestufte Freiräume. Es stellte sich heraus, dass ein Abriss der Siedlung und ihr Wiederaufbau ökonomisch und gestalterisch günstiger ist als eine aufwändige, grundlegende Ertüchtigung der Häuser.

Auch bei diesem Projekt hat ASTOC das städtebauliche Denken im größeren Maßstab geholfen, eine adäquate bauliche Lösung zu finden: Die Entwerfer gaben den Zeilen einen Knick in der Mitte, sodass je zwei dieser Zeilen zueinander und voneinander weg weisen. Dieser scheinbar ganz einfache Eingriff führt zu enormen Verbesserungen: Die Zeilenzwischenräume werden lose gefasst, ohne die Probleme der Blockrandbebauung zu schaffen. Alternierend entstehen so grüne Innenhöfe und echte, halböffentliche Höfe, die sich Bewohner und Besucher aneignen können. Die Dichte in der Siedlung konnte sogar deutlich erhöht werden, ohne dass dies unangenehm auffallen würde. Insgesamt wurden 434 Wohnungen (18 Häuser in drei Bauabschnitten) gebaut.

Statt der Satteldächer wurde eine geneigte Dachform gewählt: Der traditionell mittig sitzende Dachfirst wurde diagonal auf die jeweiligen Außenecken des Gebäudes gezogen. Dadurch entstehen die charakteristischen fallenden und steigenden Traufkanten. Um das neue Denken des Siedlungsbaus auch in einer frischeren Gestaltung zum Ausdruck zu bringen, haben alle Häuser mineralische Putzfassaden in fünf verschiedenen hellen Grüntönen. Über das gesamte Quartier verändert sich der Helligkeitswert von Nordost nach Südwest von einem hellen zu einem dunkleren Grün. Jeweils zwei Farbwerte finden sich an einem Haus. Der Wechsel befindet sich an den Hausecken und an den Knicklinien. Das nächste Gebäude nimmt einen Farbwert des benachbarten Gebäudes auf und wechselt zum nächstdunkleren Tonwert. Diese Farbgebung unterstreicht die Plastizität der Baukörper.

Obwohl die günstigen Sozialmieten erhalten bleiben konnten, gibt es Tiefgaragen mit direktem Zugang zum Gebäude. Zwei Häuser wurden mit Aufzügen ausgestattet, bei allen anderen Gebäuden können diese nachgerüstet werden. Standardmäßig werden zwei Wohnungen durch ein Treppenhaus erschlossen (Zweispänner), an den Gebäudeenden finden sich überwiegend Dreispänner. Die Größen der öffentlich geförderten Wohnungen reichen dabei von der Einzimmerwohnung bis hin zur Vierzimmerwohnung.

Das Wohnquartier wurde um belebende Infrastruktureinrichtungen ergänzt wie ein Mietercafé, quartiersnahe Büronutzungen und eine dreizügige Kindertagesstätte. Die Wohnnutzung wird bereichert durch ein Wohnheim für Menschen mit Behinderung und eine Wohngruppe für Demenzkranke.

ties as well as graded open spaces. It turned out that demolishing the complex and building anew on the site was economically and aesthetically more sensible than elaborately refurbishing the existing buildings.

Thinking on a large urban development scale has helped ASTOC find an adequate built solution: the designers introduced a bend in the middle of the rows so that two rows run towards each other while two others run away from each other. This seemingly simple intervention leads to enormous improvements: the spaces in between the rows are loosely enclosed without creating the problems associated with perimeter blocks. As such, lush courtyards and semi-public ones alternate with each other, allowing residents and visitors to appropriate them for themselves. It also became possible to significantly raise the density of the housing complex without adversely affecting its spatial qualities. In total, 434 apartments, consisting of 18 buildings constructed in three phases, were built.

Instead of gabled roofs, inclined roofs were chosen: the traditional, centrally placed roof ridge was diagonally spanned over the respective exterior corners of the building. This is what creates the characteristic falling and rising eaves. The new thinking on housing complexes has resulted in a fresh aesthetic approach, leading to the application of mineral-based plaster facades in five different light green tones. The tonal gradations are spread over the entire urban quarter, changing from a lighter green tone in the northeast to a darker green in the southwest. There are two colors on every building which change at the building's corners and on the bending lines. The building next in line takes up a color value of its neighboring building and changes to the next darker hue, underlining the plasticity of the structures.

While the low subsidized rent levels were able to be retained, the complex is able to offer dedicated underground parking facilities. Two buildings were equipped with elevators while all the other buildings have been provided with the option of retrofitting elevators. Following the standard, two apartments are accessed by one staircase (defined as a pair), while at the ends of the buildings one staircase mostly serves groups of three apartments. The sizes of the publicly funded apartments range from one-room to four-room types.

The residential quarter was supplemented by lively infrastructural facilities such as a tenants' café, office spaces that are close by, and a three-stream daycare center. Domestic life is enriched by a hall of residence for disabled people and a living group for people suffering from dementia.

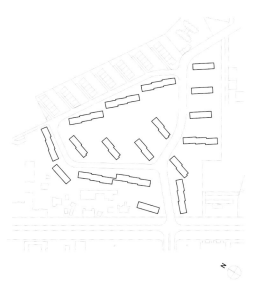

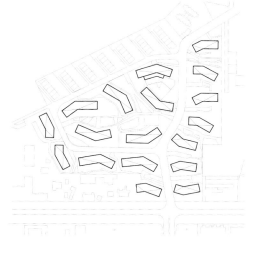

LAGEPLAN DER „ALTEN" SIEDLUNG
SITE PLAN OF THE "OLD" DEVELOPMENT

LAGEPLAN DER „NEUEN" SIEDLUNG
SITE PLAN OF THE "NEW" DEVELOPMENT

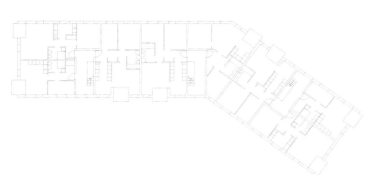

Der Entwurf für die Siedlung am Buchheimer Weg in Köln versteht sich als kritische Fortschreibung der 1950er-Jahre-Konzepte. Er beweist, dass die Lebensbedingungen in einem sozial schwierigen Stadtteil verbessert und der Nachkriegsstädtebau mit einfachen Mitteln um neue Qualitäten ergänzt werden kann. Besonders die fein abgestuften Freiräume leiten von den privaten über halböffentliche zu den öffentlichen Räumen über.

The design for the housing complex at Buchheimer Weg in Cologne represents a critical forward projection of the concepts of the nineteen-fifties. It proves that the living conditions in a socially problematic urban district can be improved and urban developments of the post-war period complemented by new qualities that employ simple methods. The delicately graded open spaces, in particular, take on a crucial role as important links between the private, semi-public and public spaces.

BÜRO- UND GESCHÄFTSHAUS
FRIESENPLATZ, KÖLN
OFFICE AND COMMERCIAL BUILDING
FRIESENPLATZ, COLOGNE

Es ist ein Missverständnis, dass „Nachhaltigkeit" ein neues Konzept oder gar eine Frage von technischen Gadgets sei: Nichts ist nachhaltiger als dichte, solide, urbane, gemischt genutzte Gebäude, deren Grundrisse so wenig determiniert sind, dass sie über Jahrzehnte hinweg die unterschiedlichsten Nutzungen zulassen. Das Wohn- und Geschäftshaus am Kölner Friesenplatz ist so ein Haus, das auch Jahrzehnte nach seiner Erstellung noch Raum für neue Ansprüche bietet, wie sein umfangreicher Umbau durch ASTOC beweist. Der Friesenplatz liegt an den Kölner Ringen und dient als Zugang zum beliebten Belgischen Viertel.

Die Substanz des in Teilen schon zu Beginn des vergangenen Jahrhunderts errichteten Büro- und Geschäftshauses, das der Rheinland-Versicherung gehört, erwies sich als grundsolide: Um mehr Licht und einen Hof als Adresse in das eng bebaute Karree zu bringen, wurden Teile der Flügel abgerissen. So konnten zusätzliche, gestaffelte Terrassenflächen gewonnen werden. Durch das Aufsetzen eines Penthousegeschosses wurde der Nutzflächenverlust

It is a misunderstanding that "sustainability" is a new concept and that it necessarily has to do with technical gadgetry: nothing is more sustainable than dense, solid, urban and mixed-use buildings whose floor plans are open and flexible to allow for the most diverse uses spread over many decades. The residential and office building at Cologne's Friesenplatz is just such a building: even decades after its construction, it provides suitable spaces for new requirements, as ASTOC's conversion has shown. The Friesenplatz square is located at the Cologne Rings. Today, the square is a lively urban space with shops and restaurants and serves as entry point to the popular Belgian Quarter.

The structure of the office building, already erected in parts at the beginning of the twentieth century and belonging to the Rheinland insurance company today, turned out to have a fundamentally solid structure. In order to bring more light into the building and include a courtyard in the densely packed square inside, parts of the wings were demolished with the result that additional, stacked terrace

ausgeglichen. Das Haus bietet heute alle Bestandteile, die eine Stadt ausmachen: 22 Wohnungen und Lofts ebenso wie Läden und Büros.

Damit sich Besucher in dem Haus leicht zurechtfinden, wurde ein Gebäudeleitsystem entwickelt, das schon auf der Platzfassade beginnt und auf römischen Zahlen basiert. Das Haus hat die Nummer „Friesen 16": Kreuz (X), Pfeil (V) und Linie (I) bilden die grafischen Bausteine für eine umfassende Signaletik mit Logo und Leitsystem sowie ein prägnantes Muster zur Gestaltung der Haupt- und Nebeneingänge.

Am Kopfbau zum Friesenplatz wurde ein zweigeschossiges neues Dachgeschoss mit Büronutzungen und einer Galerie aufgesetzt und in den zum Hof orientierten Flügeln konnten hochwertige Maisonettewohnungen – teilweise mit großartigem Blick über die Stadt Köln sowie auf den östlich gelegenen Dom – realisiert werden. In den Obergeschossen befinden sich auf der zum Friesenplatz orientierten Gebäudefront Büroräume und im Blockinneren die Wohnungen. Um in dieser gut erschlossenen Innenstadtlage Stellplätze anbieten zu können, wurde in einem Teil des entkernten Gebäudes ein vollautomatisches Parksystem eingebaut. Die Wohnungen und der sogenannte „Parksafe" werden über den innenliegenden Hof und die Büros über den Haupteingang am Friesenplatz erschlossen. Beide Erschließungen treffen sich an einer inneren Magistrale.

Um den Wohnungen in den rückwärtigen Höfen zusätzliche Attraktivität zu geben, wurden die Gebäude „zurückgeschnitten" und „zurückgestaffelt", um blickgeschützte Terrassen unterschied-

space could be added. To make up for lost area, a penthouse level was added on top. Today, the building offers all the amenities of vibrant urban life: twenty-two apartments and lofts, as well as shops and offices.

An orientation system was developed to aid visitors find their way through the building. It begins right at the facade facing the square and is based on Roman numerals. The building has the number "Friesen 16". Crosses (X), arrows (V), and lines (I) make up the graphic elements for a comprehensive signage system with a logo and a guiding system as well as a distinctive pattern for the design of the main and side entrances.

The front section facing Friesenplatz was extended to accommodate a new two-storied roof level with offices and a gallery on top. In the wings facing the courtyard, exclusive duplex apartments, some of them offering magnificent views of the city and of Cologne Cathedral located further east, have been built. The upper floors house offices in the part that faces the Friesenplatz square, while the apartments are located on the interior sides. Parking in this well-connected inner city location was made possible by the inclusion of a fully automated parking system in a part of the de-cored building. The apartments and the parking facility are accessed via the inside courtyard, while the offices are reached via the main entrance located on Friesenplatz. Both access routes meet along another path inside.

In order to make the apartments in the rear-facing courtyards even more attractive, the buildings were set and stacked back, creat-

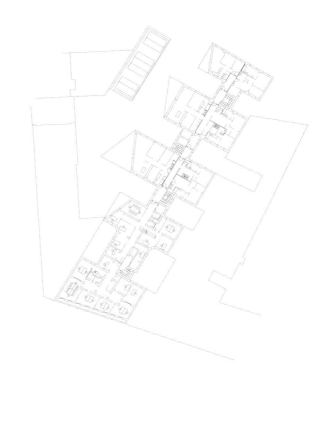

Höhe zu schaffen: ein Akt der „urbanen Akupunktur". Wie attraktiv solche städtischen Höfe sein können, hat die Renaissance der Hackeschen Höfe in Berlin zuletzt eindrucksvoll gezeigt. Das Haus am Friesenplatz beweist, wie ein gemischt genutztes Haus als Mikrokosmos der Stadt über viele Jahrzehnte ökologisch und ökonomisch „nachhaltig" bleiben kann: Ein gelungener Beitrag zur Wandlungsfähigkeit von städtischen Gebäuden.

ing private terraces of varying heights and representing a kind of "urban acupuncture." How attractive such urban courtyards can become was impressively demonstrated by the renaissance of the Hackeschen Höfe in Berlin. The building at Friesenplatz has shown how a mixed-use building can remain ecologically and economically "sustainable," becoming a microcosm of the city over many decades. It represents a successful contribution to the versatility of inner-city architecture.

WOHNEN HERTI 6, ZUG, SCHWEIZ (CH)
HOUSING AT HERTI 6, ZUG, SWITZERLAND (CH)

Die Stadt Zug ist selbst für die hohen Schweizer Maßstäbe etwas Besonderes: In dieser kleinen Stadt am Zuger See gibt es mehr Firmen als Einwohner. Angelockt von den niedrigen Steuersätzen, die 1946 eingeführt wurden, hat die Einrichtung Tausender Briefkastenfirmen und Holdings der Stadt in den letzten drei Jahrzehnten einen gehörigen Wachstumsschub beschert, der in der engen Altstadt keinen Raum fand. Zug ist zugleich der kleinste und reichste Kanton. Heute leben etwa 114.000 Menschen in Zug, die Bevölkerung hat sich in den letzten 40 Jahren verdoppelt. Das Herti genannte Areal verdankt seinen ungewöhnlichen Namen dem Wort „Härte" – des lehmigen Bodens und der harten Arbeit, die Landwirtschaft auf ihm erfordert. Es liegt westlich der Innenstadt und wurde deshalb in den letzten Jahrzehnten zu einem neuen, modernen Stadtteil entwickelt, der die Altstadt flächenmäßig in den Schatten stellt und zugleich entlastet. Gleich mehrere Hochhäuser wachsen derzeit über der Silhouette der mittelalterlichen Stadt. Die Herti wirkt wie ein Open-Air-Museum der städtebaulichen Vorstellungen in der Schweiz seit dem Zweiten Weltkrieg: Biedere Satteldach-Zeilen in den 1950er Jahren im ersten Bauabschnitt, gefolgt von nutzungsentmischten Waschbeton-Riesen der 60er und 70er Jahre in den Phasen Zwei, Drei und Vier, bis hin zu Stahl-Glasgehäusen, wie sie typisch für die 80er Jahre waren, im fünften Bauabschnitt. 1976 wurde eine Schule gebaut, 1983 ein Einkaufszentrum, 1967 eine Sporthalle und 1984 ein Altersheim. Heute ist die Herti damit fast eine autarke Stadt. All diesen „städtebaulichen Sedimenten" ist gemein, dass sie im Auftrag oder auf dem Bauland der „Korporation

The town of Zug is special, even by the high Swiss standards: this small town at the shores of Lake Zug is home to more companies than it is to people. Ever since 1946, when low taxes were introduced, the town has attracted a growing number of letterbox and holding companies, leading to strong growth in the last three decades which has, in turn, led to a scarcity of space in the old part of town. Zug is both the smallest and the wealthiest canton of Switzerland. Today, around 114,000 people live in Zug. The population has doubled in the last forty years. The Herti area, somewhat unusually named after "Härte" (German for "hardness"), recalls the clay-rich soil and the hard work that went into plowing the land. The area conveniently lies west of the town center, leading to its development into a modern urban district over the last couple of decades. It is an area that dwarfs the old town by its sheer size, while it also relieves the old center. Several high-rise buildings currently rise above the silhouette of the medieval town. The Herti area seems to represent an open-air museum collection of all the urban planning concepts that have been applied in Switzerland since World War Two: there are conventional-looking rows of gabled roofs dating from the first building phase in the nineteen-fifties, followed by mono-functional behemoths of exposed aggregate concrete from the second, third and fourth building phases in the sixties and seventies. Then steel-and-glass buildings typical of the eighties can be found, dating from the fifth phase. A school was built in 1976, a shopping center in 1983, a gymnasium in 1967, and a senior citizens' home in 1984. As such, Herti is almost a self-sufficient town today. What all these ur-

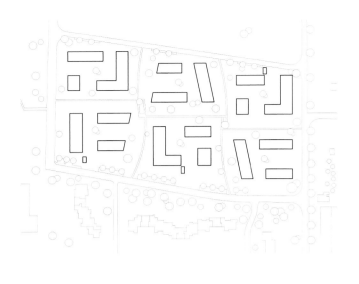

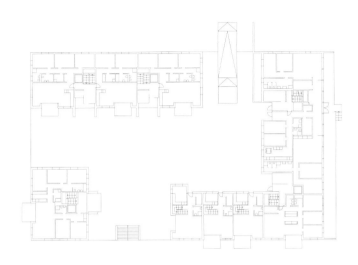

Zug" gebaut wurden. Diese Institution hält in Zug wichtige Zügel in der Hand: Ihr gehören große Wald- und Feldflächen und damit auch das entscheidende Bauland, das Zug für seine Weiterentwicklung dringend benötigt. Die „Korporation Zug" ist eine öffentlich-rechtliche Körperschaft, die aus Nachfahren von 36 Zuger „Geschlechtern" besteht. Dazu gehören heute circa 4500 Personen. Die Korporation behält den Grund und gibt lediglich das Baurecht an weitere Investoren ab.

Am nördlichen Rand der Stadt sollte der Bauabschnitt „Herti 6" nach einem Entwurf von ASTOC als „Mittler zwischen Stadt und Lorzenebene" dienen. Der städtebauliche Entwurf sieht sechs Wohnhöfe vor, die jeweils auf einem gemeinsamen Plateau stehen. In den Höfen Zwei, Vier und Sechs ist stets ein Gebäude Punkt-, eines Riegel- und eines L-förmig. Die Höfe Eins, Drei und Fünf bestehen aus jeweils drei Riegeln. Während der fließende öffentliche Raum in der benachbarten 70er-Jahre-Siedlung keinen Halt findet und wie Abstandsgrün wirkt, schaffen die Wohnhöfe Nachbarschaften und lesbare Räume, sowohl im inneren und äußeren Straßenraum. Miet- und Eigentumswohnungen wurden gemischt, ebenso geförderter und frei finanzierter Wohnungsbau. Alle Wohnungen sind für Familien konzipiert und entsprechend groß.

ban planning "layers" have in common is the fact that they were all commissioned by or built on land owned by the "Korporation Zug". This institution has been and continues to be highly influential in Zug. It owns large forest and agricultural tracts and hence also key building land which the town urgently needs for its further development. The "Korporation Zug" is a public corporation made up of the descendants of thirty-six "dynasties" of Zug which include around 4,500 people today. The corporation retains ownership of the land and extends building rights only to potential new investors.

At the northern end of the town, the "Herti 6" building phase, planned by ASTOC, has been planned to function as a mediator between the city and the Lorzenebene. The new city plan envisages six residential courtyard units that together stand on one plateau. In courtyard units two, four, and six, one building is always either point-shaped, oblong, or L-shaped. Courtyard units one, three and five each consist of three oblong buildings. While the free-flowing public space seems disjointed in the neighboring housing estate dating from the seventies, appearing more like a distanced green buffer zone, the courtyard units create true neighborhoods and legible spaces, both inside as well as outside in the space of the street. Rented and freehold apartments have been spatially mixed,

Die Wohnhöfe Eins bis Vier sind bereits 2005 erstellt worden und bieten 150 Miet- und 46 Eigentumswohnungen, teils als Maisonetten gestaltet, sowie eine Kindertagesstätte. Die Wohnhöfe Fünf und Sechs bieten je 48 Mietwohnungen im Minergie-Standard – Minergie ist der wichtigste Energiestandard in der Schweiz für Niedrigenergiehäuser – und eine weitere Kindertagesstätte.

Außen sind die sechs Blöcke weiß gestaltet. Sie zeigen nur zum Innenhof und an den Fassaden der zurückspringenden Geschosse ihre Farbigkeit und Materialität. Die ein- und zweigeschossigen Staffelgeschosse sind in unterschiedlichen Farbtönen gestaltet und mal mit Faserzementplatten, mal mit Holz in verschiedenen Formaten und Mustern verkleidet über einem gemeinsamen Sockel mit Putzfassade. Der erhöhte Hof bietet einen geschützten Bereich mit Spielflächen für kleine Kinder. Jeder Hof wurde unterschiedlich gestaltet. Im Zentrum der Höfe steht jeweils ein Baum in einem Patio (mit Verbindung zur Tiefgarage), über dessen Öffnung die Parkebene natürlich belichtet und belüftet wird. Sickerflächen fangen das Regenwasser an Ort und Stelle auf und machen es erlebbar. Von der Straße aus führt eine Rampe hinauf in den Hof und eine hinab in die nur halb versenkte Parkebene. Alle Hauseingänge liegen zum Hof hin. Im Wohnhof Zwei wurden die Hausnummern als große,

so too sponsored and self-financed housing. All apartments have been designed for families and are appropriately sized.

Courtyard units one to four were already built in 2005 and offer 150 rented and forty-eight freehold apartments, partly designed as duplex types, while also providing a day-care center. Courtyard units five and six each provide 48 rented apartments conforming to the Minergie standard which is the most important energy standard for low-energy buildings in Switzerland. These units also house another day-care center.

On the outside, the six building blocks are white. They show their colorfulness and materiality only in the inner courtyards and on the façades of the set back floors. The single- and double-story stacked floors have each been colored differently, clad in either fiber cement slabs or wood of varying sizes and textures, supported by a common base with a plaster façade. A raised courtyard provides protected space with playing areas for small children. Each courtyard has been differently designed. A tree has been planted in a patio in the center of each courtyard, also providing a link to the underground garage which is naturally lit and ventilated by the patio. Drainage surfaces catch rainwater on the spot, turning it into a tangible spatial experience. From the street a ramp leads up to the

farbige Skulpturen gestaltet und im Wohnhof Sechs bildet ein Becken mit Wasser und Sand ein einzigartiges Spielgelände für die Kinder. Jede Hofgestaltung ist individuell und bildet so eine eigene Identität. Die Wohnungen verfügen über Freiflächen nach Süden, Westen und Osten, die halb Loggia und halb Balkon sind. Die Fenster „springen" von Etage zu Etage ein wenig, um den Fassaden eine spielerische Note zu geben.

Der Entwurf für den neuesten Bauteil der Siedlung Herti 6 in Zug zeigt exemplarisch, welche hohen Qualitäten stadtnahes, familienfreundliches Wohnen heute bieten kann.

courtyard while another one leads down to the semi-sunk parking level. All entrances are oriented towards the courtyard. In courtyard unit two the house numbers have been designed as large, colorful sculptures, while in courtyard unit six a pool of water and sand forms part of a unique playing ground for children. Each courtyard unit has been individually designed and has its distinct identity. The apartments have open spaces directed towards the south, west and east, designed to be part loggia and part balcony. The windows are each recessed slightly differently on the floor levels to lend the façade a playful note. The design of this newest built addition to the housing estate of Herti in Zug exemplifies how family-oriented housing that is simultaneously close to city life can provide a truly high-quality living environment.

HOFQUARTIER, HAFENCITY HAMBURG
HOUSING DEVELOPMENT, HAFENCITY HAMBURG

Um in der Hamburger HafenCity auch günstigere Wohnungen anbieten zu können, wurde am Dalmannkai, südöstlich des Sandtorparks, ein geschlossener Block mit erschwinglichen Wohnhäusern geplant und gebaut. Zwischen einer Schule und einem Kraftwerk am Magdeburger Hafen gelegen, sollten ursprünglich vier bis fünf Wohnhäuser auf kleinen Parzellen gebaut werden, die das preisliche Spektrum für Wohnungen in der HafenCity erweitern. Weil die örtliche Baupolitik zugleich Baugruppen fördern wollte, wurde das Grundstück („Baufeld 4") in nur zwei Teile geteilt: Die östliche Hälfte wurde einer Baugruppe zugeschlagen (Entwurf: Iris Neitmann, Hamburg) und für die westliche wurde von ASTOC ein siebenstöckiges Wohn- und Geschäftshaus geplant. Das Haus illustriert als Bautyp die städtebaulichen Leitvorstellungen von ASTOC für diesen Teil der HafenCity: Im Erdgeschoss gibt es einen Laden und vier zweigeschossige Home-Office-Lofts, in denen Selbständige leben und arbeiten können. In den vier Etagen darüber liegen je vier Wohnungen, die als Zweispänner organisiert sind. Der Grundriss erlaubt es, dass die Schlafräume nach Norden zum Hof und die Wohnräume nach Süden zur Straße hin orientiert werden können. Die Eigentumswohnungen sind zumeist um die 60–80 Quadratmeter groß und haben damit genau die richtige Größe für Singles oder Paare und bleiben dennoch bezahlbar. Da es nur wenige tragende Wände gibt, konnte der Innenausbau sehr individuell erfolgen. Die obersten beiden Etagen bieten große Penthouse-Wohnungen über zwei Stockwerke. Zur Straße hin präsentiert sich das Haus mit einer einfachen Lochfassade, die durch die verschiedenen Farben der verwendeten Ziegel lebendig wirkt.

Die Wohnbebauung hat gezeigt, wie dringend Städtebau Koordination benötigt. Auch wenn sich nicht alle Vorstellungen vom bürgerlichen Bauen auf kleinen Parzellen durchsetzen ließen, so orientiert sich der Entwurf dennoch an seinen Nachbarn: Einem Wohnhaus vom Büro KBNK (Kähne Birwe Krause Nähring) aus Hamburg, mit dem es eine gemeinsame Tiefgarage teilt, und der nahen Katharinen-Schule von Spengler & Wiescholek, Hamburg.

With the objective to add more affordable apartments to the housing mix at Hamburg's HafenCity, a closed building block with low-priced apartments were planned and built at Dalmannkai, southeast of the Sandtorpark. Located between a school and a power station at the Magdeburg Port, the original idea was to construct four to five apartment buildings on small plots, thereby extending the price range of apartments in the HafenCity. As the local building policy encouraged the formation of building groups, the plot (called Baufeld 4) was divided into two parts only: the eastern half was added to a building group (design: Iris Neitmann, Hamburg) while the western half was planned to accommodate a seven-story residential and office building, designed by ASTOC. As a specific building typology, it is a good example of ASTOC's urban planning principles as applied to this part of the HafenCity: the first floor houses a shop and four double-story home office lofts where self-employed people can live and work. The four upper levels each accommodate four paired apartments. The ground plan allows the bedrooms to be orientated to the north, facing the courtyard, while the living rooms point to the south, facing the street. The free-hold apartments are mostly between sixty and eighty square meters in size, being ideal for singles or couples while remaining affordable. As there are only few load-bearing walls, the interior design was able to cater to a wide range of individual tastes. The two uppermost levels house large penthouse apartments spread over two stories. A simple perforated facade faces the street which seems to come alive with the different colors of the brick used in its construction.

This housing development has shown how urgent the application of good coordination is to urban planning. Even if all the expectations of middle-class building construction cannot be met on small plots, this particular design has been able to provide high quality, taking inspiration from its neighboring buildings which include an apartment building, designed by Hamburg-based KBNK (Kähne Birwe Krause Nähring), with a shared underground garage, and the nearby Katharinen School, designed by Spengler & Wiescholek from Hamburg.

WOHNEN GRUBE CARL, FRECHEN
HOUSING IN THE FORMER COAL MINE "CARL", FRECHEN

Die Grube Carl in Frechen gehört zu einem Ring von Braunkohlegruben südwestlich der Stadt Köln. Sie war von 1907–1995 in Betrieb. Die Firma Rheinbraun AG hatte die Grube in Benzelrath 1905–1907 erbaut. Es ist die letzte erhaltene Anlage ihres Alters in der Bundesrepublik. Die ehemalige Brikettfabrik ist heute denkmalgeschützt, sodass der Produktionsablauf ablesbar bleiben kann: Ehemals wurde hier Braunkohle per Bahn angeliefert, befeuchtet und verarbeitet. Die gesamte Anlage liegt auf einem Plateau und dominiert mit ihren Schloten und Dachaufbauten die Silhouette der Gegend. Die Schlote wurden erhalten und werden nun abends stimmungsvoll illuminiert.

Ausgehend von der Prämisse, dass fortgesetzte Nutzung der beste Denkmalschutz ist und angesichts der Tatsache, dass die Gegend um Rhein und Ruhr bereits reich an Industriedenkmalen ist, wurde die Fabrik zu einer außergewöhnlichen Wohnanlage umgebaut. Von zehn Fabrikgebäuden wurden sechs erhalten. Die Gebäude „Pressenhaus", „Nassdienst", „Elektrostation" und „Niederdruckkesselhaus" wurden zu Loftwohnungen umgebaut. Sie erhielten neue Dächer, restaurierte Fassaden und sind durch die prägnanten Bandbrücken verbunden. Die Außenanlagen wurden ebenfalls neu gestaltet.

Architektonisch zielt der Umbau nicht auf ein High-End-Design, sondern auf komfortables, bezahlbares Wohnen mit einmaliger Atmosphäre. Die Gebäude auf dem Grubengelände haben ganz unterschiedliche Maßstäbe. Die ehemalige Werkstatthalle wurde zu Townhouses mit Parkgaragen. Dafür mussten lediglich „Kerne", also Treppen und Aufzüge, eingefügt werden. In das ehemalige Trocken- und Pressenhaus wurden große Wohnungen eingebaut, die flexibel in der Aufteilung sind und große Stahlbalkone oder bis zu 65 Quadratmeter große Dachterrassen haben. In Frechen kann man stadtnah wohnen und dennoch weite Blicke in die umgebende Natur genießen. In den obersten Geschossen wurden Maisonettes gebaut, mehrheitlich als Eigentumswohnungen. Ihre expressive Dachland-

The coal mine "Carl" in Frechen is part of a ring of coal mines located southwest of the city of Cologne. In operation between 1907 and 1995, it was built by the Rheinbraun AG company in Benzelrath in 1905–1907. Today, it represents the last conserved facility of its kind in Germany. The former briquette factory is a listed site today, making its previous production process wonderfully legible in the present. In earlier times, brown coal was delivered to the site by train where it was moisturized and processed. The entire facility lies on a raised plateau and dominates the skyline of the area with its chimneys and roof structures. The chimneys have been conserved and are now elegantly illuminated after dark.

Following the maxim that the best way to go about built heritage conservation is to ensure continued use, and considering the fact that the area around the Rhine and Ruhr Rivers has a wealth of industrial monuments, the factory has been converted into a unique new housing complex. From a total of ten factory buildings, six have been conserved. The buildings "Pressenhaus", "Nassdienst", "Elektrostation", and "Niederdruckkesselhaus", have been converted into loft apartments. Furnished with new roofs and restored facades, they are connected with each other by the site's distinctive conveyor bridges. The outside facilities have also been redesigned. In architectural terms, the conversion was not intended to be a high-end design, but rather provide comfortable and affordable housing in a unique atmosphere. The buildings on the coal mine site have very different scales: the former workshop hall was converted into townhouses and a parking garage. All that this required was the addition of staircases and elevators, collectively comprising the so-called "cores" of the buildings. In the former drying and pressing building, large apartments have been accommodated that can be flexibly divided, providing generous steel balconies or sixty-five square meter roof terraces. In Frechen, it is possible to live close to the city and still enjoy magnificent views of the surrounding countryside. The uppermost floors house duplex apartments,

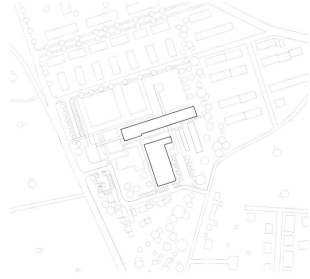

schaft nutzt die ehemaligen Ablufthauben der Grube. Die Kontur der Dachaufbauten konnte erhalten werden. Sehr unterschiedliche Deckenhöhen von bis zu 4,50 Meter geben den Wohnungen ein außergewöhnliches Raumgefühl. In weiteren Gebäuden entstanden zehn Stadthäuser sowie Gewerbe- und Büroeinheiten. In einer ehemaligen Lagerhalle wurde eine „Parkpalette" eingebaut.

Eine neu eingerichtete „Denkmalachse" wurde als Reminiszenz an die Industriegeschichte des Ortes angelegt und führt von der ältesten Brikettpresse zum Trocken- und Pressenhaus. Als offener Durchgang zwischen zwei Stadträumen verknüpft sie den nördlichen und südlichen Teil des Quartiers und macht Industriekultur erlebbar.

Der Umbau erfolgte sensibel und in mehreren Bauabschnitten. Das Konzept erwies sich als sehr erfolgreich und wurde so zu einem guten Beispiel für eine nachhaltige Stadtentwicklung, die historisch Überkommenem neue Qualitäten abgewinnt.

mostly as freehold property. The former suction hoods of the coal mine produce an expressive roof landscape. The contours of the roof structures have been conserved. Different ceiling heights of up to 4.5 meters lend the apartments an extraordinary feeling of space. Ten townhouses have been accommodated in other buildings which also house commercial and office facilities. A former warehouse was converted into a parking deck.

A new "heritage axis" was also designed in reminder of the industrial history of the place, leading from the oldest briquette press to the drying and pressing building. Conceived as an open passage in between two urban spaces, it connects the northern and southern parts of the quarter with each other, making its former industrial culture tangible. The conversion was sensitively implemented and took place in several building phases. The concept has proven to be highly successful and has become a good example of sustainable urban development that strives to infuse new qualities into otherwise defunct historical buildings.

WERBEAGENTUR „MILK", KÖLN
ADVERTISING AGENCY "MILK", COLOGNE

Direkt an einer aufgegebenen Bahnlinie gelegen, wartete ein ehemaliges Generatorenhaus der Deutschen Bahn darauf, aus seinem Dornröschenschlaf wachgeküsst zu werden. Nach einem Entwurf von ASTOC wurde das gründerzeitliche Nutzgebäude durch eine L-förmige Aufstockung zu einem modernen Lofthaus mit Atmosphäre umgebaut. Die Nutzfläche wurde dabei verdoppelt. Das entwurfliche Thema war „Alt und Neu": Ziel des Entwurfs war es nicht, ein auf Hochglanz poliertes, schickes Bürohaus zu bauen, das auch gar nicht in dieses raue Umfeld passen würde. Die Architekten haben das Haus zunächst selbst genutzt, dann nach ihrem Auszug den An- und Umbau auf die Bedürfnisse des neuen Nutzers maßgeschneidert angepasst. Heute dient das Haus einer Werbeagentur mit dem Namen „Milk". Das zusammengesetzte Gebäude sollte etwas Widersprüchliches behalten. Der Höhenversprung in dem Gebäude zeigt sich auch in der Fassade. Ebenso wie der Altbau beruht auch der Neubau auf einer offen sichtbaren Stahlkonstruktion, die sich unverkleidet in den jeweiligen Interieurs zeigt.

Situated directly adjacent to a railroad line, a former generator building of the German Railways (Deutsche Bahn), was waiting to be kissed awake to start a new life. Following the completion of a design by ASTOC, this old utility building dating from the Wilhelminian period was converted into a modern, attractive loft by adding an L-shaped extension that doubled its usable area. Applying the motto of combining "the old and the new," the designers did not attempt to produce a fancy and highly polished office building which would be unfit for these rugged industrial surroundings in any case. The architects themselves were the first users of the building. After moving out, they adapted the extension and conversion to suit the unique requirements of the new user. Today, the building houses the advertising agency "Milk". The idea was to retain a contradictory flair in the building, creating a sense of suspense. The facade reflects the height differential in the building. Just like the old building, the new one rests on an exposed steel structure which is unclad and also visible in the interiors.

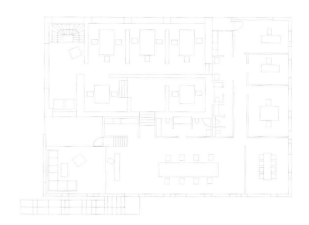

BÜROGEBÄUDE VIEGA ATTENDORN
OFFICE BUILDING FOR VIEGA ATTENDORN

Die Stärke der deutschen Wirtschaft liegt in der Vielzahl kleinerer und mittelgroßer Unternehmen, die – auch wenn sie keine weltbekannten Markenartikler sind – in ihrer Branche zu den Marktführern gehören. Die bodenständige, in der vierten Generation familiengeführte Firma Viega ist dafür ein gutes Beispiel. Ihr Stammsitz liegt versteckt, aber pittoresk in dem Örtchen Attendorn im tiefsten Sauerland in Westfalen. Die Firma stellt Produkte für die Installationstechnik her und ist in den letzten Jahrzehnten kontinuierlich gewachsen.

Der Entwurf von ASTOC für den Um- und Neubau der Firmenzentrale ging als erster Preis aus einem gewonnenen Gutachterverfahren hervor. Am Hauptsitz in Attendorn hatte das Wachstum baulich zu einem Firmensitz geführt, der seine „Jahresringe" aus Büros, Forschung und Produktion rund um die Fabrikantenvilla als Keimzelle zeigt und der – da sich die Anforderungen ständig wandeln – erweitert und dabei grundlegend umstrukturiert werden musste. Die Produktion wurde vor die Tore der Stadt verlagert.

Dem Werksgelände fehlte es bis dato an einer baulichen Mitte und einer architektonischen Identität. Es gab kein markantes Entree, kein „Herz" und auch kaum einladende Räume. Der Neubau schafft nun zugleich erstmals eine architektonisch formulierte Mitte, aber auch einen „Eingang zur Stadt" und fungiert mit seinen zahlreichen Anschlussstellen an die verschiedenen Bestandsgebäude wie ein Gelenk. Es gleicht damit einem Bestandteil der Leitungssysteme, die Viega groß gemacht haben.

Der integrierende Neubau vernetzt die bestehenden Gebäude räumlich und funktional. Neben einer kommunikativen und flexiblen Bürostruktur für 350 Mitarbeiter entstanden Veranstaltungs- und Schulungsräume sowie ein Mitarbeiterrestaurant und ein neuer Vorstandsbereich. Ein glasüberdachtes Atrium mit einer geschwungenen, frei stehenden Stahl-Wendeltreppe bietet vielfältige Sichtbeziehungen und ist auch selber ein attraktiver Blickpunkt. Das neue Verbindungsbauwerk dient als „Kopf und Rückgrat" und

One of the strengths of the German economy lies in the large number of small and medium-sized enterprises. Although they may not be behind world-famous brand names they are very much market leaders in their respective fields. A good example is Viega, a down-to-earth company that is family-run and now already in its fourth generation. Its headquarters is charmingly hidden in the small town of Attendorn, deep inside the Sauerland region of Westfalen. The company produces installation technology components and has grown continuously over the last decades.

ASTOC's design for the conversion and the new building of the company's existing headquarters was chosen as first prize in a competition. At its headquarters in Attendorn, steady growth and changing requirements led to ever-increasing "layers" of office, research and production space to be added around the centrally placed villa, just like annual rings are added to a tree, with the result that the headquarters were thoroughly restructured. The production facilities were shifted to the outskirts of the town.

What the business premises were missing were an architectural center and identity, a distinctive entrance, a striking heart and a greater number of inviting spaces. The new building, for the first time, provides a spatial and architectural center, while at the same time creates a new entry point to the city, acting as a central joint that connects the various facilities of the premises with each other. In its function, it resembles the joints of the piping systems that have made Viega famous.

The integrative new building links the existing buildings spatially and functionally with each other. Apart from a communicative and flexible office structure for 350 employees, event and training spaces have been built, as well as a staff restaurant and a new management wing. A glazed atrium with a curving, free-standing spiral staircase of steel opens up diverse visual relationships and has itself become an attractive focus. The new link building serves as the new head and spine of the premises and also makes possible

ermöglicht Anschlüsse an die unterschiedlichen Höhenniveaus der Altbauten. Die Büroflure führen in sanften Bögen vom Neubau in die Bestandsflächen.

Der Neubau verleiht dem Gebäudekomplex auch „Herz und Gesicht": Hier wurden die repräsentativen und öffentlichkeitswirksamen Nutzungen wie Foyer, Ausstellungsfläche mit Cafeteria und Geschäftsleitung angesiedelt.

Die stark vertikal geprägte Fassade erinnert an einen Strichcode und präsentiert sich in breiter Front zur Stadt. Die phasenweise Realisierbarkeit und Erweiterbarkeit war bei der Planung entscheidend. Der Neubau bietet ein hohes Maß an Vertikal-Erschließung, die Treppenhauskerne sind so angeordnet, dass in folgenden Bauabschnitten weitere Büroflügel mühelos angefügt werden können. Die Einzelbüros sind elegant gestaltet und modern ausgestattet. Zum komfortablen Arbeiten tragen ein effektiver Schallschutz und eine gute Akustik, Tageslicht und ein effektiver Blendschutz bei. Die gläsernen Wände zum Flur verleihen dem Neubau insgesamt eine hohe Transparenz. Eine Bauteilaktivierung erlaubt es, dass auf eine Klimatisierung der Büros verzichtet werden konnte.

Das neue zentrale Gebäude fördert die Kommunikation und Zirkulation zwischen den Abteilungen und in den alltäglichen Arbeitsabläufen.

various linkages to the old buildings located at different heights. The office corridors are gently curved, leading from the new building to the existing areas.

The new building also lends the premises a new heart and a new face, housing representative public spaces such as a foyer, an exhibition space, a cafeteria and the senior management section.

The strong vertical orientation of the facade recalls the image of a barcode, displaying itself prominently to the town. An important feature of the building is the option it provides for phased construction and extensibility. The new building offers excellent vertical access links while the staircase cores have been built so as to allow future office wings to be easily added to the ensemble if needed. Single-occupancy offices are elegantly styled and equipped with state-of-the-art facilities. Effective soundproofing, excellent acoustics, day-lighting, and practical glare shades ensure a comfortable working atmosphere. The glazed walls leading to the corridor lend a high degree of transparency to the entire new building. An installed component activation system means that office air-conditioning could be dispensed with.

The new central building excellently promotes communication and circulation between the various sections and during daily office routines.

KASINO AN EINEM FORSCHUNGSSTANDORT IN KÖLN
CASINO AT A RESEARCH CENTER IN COLOGNE

Auf dem weitläufigen und von seiner Nachbarschaft abgeriegelten Campus stehen die einzelnen Gebäude der Institute, gehalten nur durch ihre Infrastruktur, sonst völlig losgelöst: Der Gestaltung dieses sozialen Mittelpunkts kommt also große Bedeutung zu. Der welkende Bau aus den 1970er Jahren musste dringend erweitert und saniert werden, um hochwertige und gesunde Ernährungskonzepte umsetzen zu können. Der Entwurf von ASTOC zeugt vom Respekt gegenüber den Sichtbetonfassaden der 1970er Jahre, wie

A spacious campus, sealed off from its neighborhood, houses the individual buildings of seven institutes which appear to stand scattered on the site, held together only by their common institutional infrastructure. As such, the design of this social focus assumes great importance. The fading building dating from the seventies had to be urgently extended and renovated, to offer high-quality and healthy nutrition concepts. ASTOC's design respectfully treats the exposed concrete facades of the old building from the seventies,

sie den Altbau prägen, findet aber dennoch eine unmissverständlich zeitgenössische Architektursprache für den Anbau. Die schwere Bestandsfassade konnte energetisch optimiert und dennoch in ihrer ursprünglichen Anmutung erhalten werden. Die pigmentierten Sichtbetonplatten des Bestandsgebäudes wurden für den Erweiterungsbau nachproduziert, die bestehende Fassade wird nachträglich gedämmt. Die Betonoberflächen zeigen die „Handwerklichkeit" der Holzlatten-Schalung.

but at the same time, is unmistakably contemporary in its architectural expression for the extension building. The heavy facade of the existing building was energetically optimized while preserving its original appearance. Its pigmented exposed concrete slabs were reproduced for the extension building while the existing facade will later be insulated. The concrete surfaces clearly show the craftsmanship-like traces of the wooden formwork.

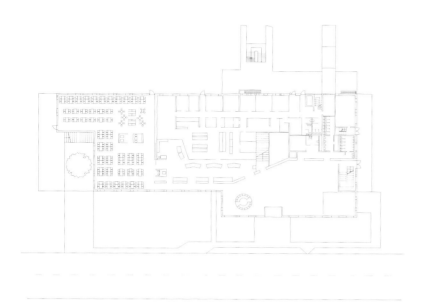

Der eingeschossige Anbau nimmt den Speisesaal und die neue Großküche auf, sodass im Obergeschoss des Altbaus Platz für einen großen Veranstaltungssaal frei wird. Im neuen Kasino können nicht nur täglich circa 700 Mahlzeiten serviert werden, es gibt auch eine Dachterrasse und ein Gründach.

Der Umbau des Kasinos ist ein Beispiel für den zeitgemäßen Weiterbau eines Gebäudes aus einer anderen Ära, bei dem sich Respekt vor der Baugeschichte und ein selbstbewusster, zeitgenössischer Entwurf nicht ausschließen.

The single-story extension houses the dining hall and the new canteen kitchen, freeing space for a large event hall on the upper floor of the old building. Not only is the new casino capable of preparing and serving around 700 meals daily, it can also boast of a roof terrace and a green roof.

The conversion of the casino is a good example for the contemporary extension of a building from another era, exemplifying a respectful treatment of building history within a confidently inspiring and modern design.

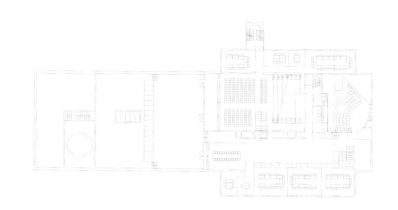

ERWEITERUNG DER ABTEI HAMBORN, DUISBURG
EXTENSION OF HAMBORN ABBEY, DUISBURG

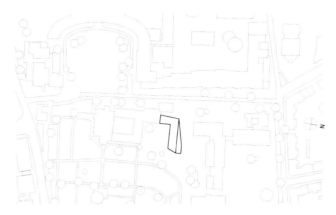

Florierendes katholisches Klosterleben vermutet man nicht gerade in einer industriell geprägten Stadt wie Duisburg. Aber der Ortsteil Hamborn ist anders als die von der welkenden Schwerindustrie dominierten Stadtbezirke. An der Stelle, an der heute die Abtei St. Johann steht, wurde Hamborn schon vor mehr als tausend Jahren besiedelt. Die geistliche Geschichte begann mit der Schenkung des Gutshofs Hamborn an den Kölner Erzbischof im Jahr 1136 mit der Auflage, dort ein Kloster zu errichten. Die kleine Pfarrkirche, die auf dem Gutshof schon im 9. Jahrhundert errichtet worden war, wurde also zur Klosterkirche umgebaut. Zur Verbindung mit den Klostergebäuden wurde ein romanischer Kreuzgang angefügt, von dem heute noch der Nordflügel besteht. Die Klosterkirche wurde 1170 geweiht, das Kloster zur Abtei erhoben. 1806 in der Säkularisation aufgehoben, im Zweiten Weltkrieg zum großen Teil zerstört, wurde das Kloster 1959 von sieben Mitbrüdern neu besiedelt und 1994 wieder zur Abtei erhoben. 1974 erfolgte ein dreigeschossiger Anbau als Erweiterung der Klosteranlage mit Wohn- und Büroräumen nach dem Entwurf des Kölner Architekten Hans Schilling.

Heute gehören der Abtei 25 Chorherren an. Da es in Hamborn Jahr für Jahr Ordensnachwuchs gibt, wurde ein weiterer Erweiterungsbau nötig. Der Bauherr wollte „communio ad intra et ad extra", „Gemeinschaft nach innen und außen", also das Typische eines Chorherrenklosters, auch in der Architektur erkennbar werden lassen. Der Entwurf von ASTOC folgt den Prinzipien der Prämonstratenser,

It may come as a surprise to find a flourishing catholic monastery in the midst of an industrial city like Duisburg. The urban district of Hamborn is, however, rather different from the ones dominated by fading heavy industry. The site of the present St. Johann Abbey in Hamborn was already settled more than a thousand years ago. The beginnings of its ecclesiastical history are marked by the donation of the Hamborn estate to the archbishop of Cologne in 1136 with the condition to build a monastery there. The small parish church, already existing on the estate since the ninth century, was subsequently converted to a monastery church. A Romanesque cloister was added to link the various buildings of the abbey with each other of which the northern wing still exists today. The monastery church was consecrated in 1170, elevating it to the status of an abbey. That title was annulled in 1806 in the course of the secularization drive. During World War Two, the buildings were largely destroyed but, as if in defiance, resettled by seven brothers in 1959. In 1994, the building complex regained the status of an abbey. In 1974, a three-storied extension was added to provide residential and office space, designed by the Cologne-based architect Hans Schilling.

Today, twenty-five canons are part of the abbey. As the order in Hamborn keeps growing each year, another building extension was required. The client wanted the architecture to express one of the typical ideals of a canonical monastery, namely that of "communio ad intra et ad extra" ("community inside and community outside"). ASTOC's design follows the principles of the Premonstensians

die ganz bewusst und gewollt das klösterliche Gemeinschaftsleben mit dem seelsorglich-missionarischen Dienst verbinden, Gemeinschaft nach innen und außen bauen wollen.

Der neue Riegel schließt einen zuvor nur auf zwei Seiten gefassten Gartenhof auf der dritten Seite. Er fügt den heterogenen Nachbarbauten einen selbstbewussten zeitgenössischen Bau hinzu. Dieser übernimmt das Prinzip der durch Stützen gesäumten Flurbereiche aus dem mittelalterlichen Flügel und dem Anbau von Hans Schilling. Wie gefaltet wirkt die unregelmäßige Geometrie des weiß verputzten Neubaus. Durch die Faltungen reagiert der Baukörper subtil auf die städtebaulichen und geometrischen Vorgaben, die sich aus dem Grundstückszuschnitt und den Anschlusshöhen der umgebenden Bestandsbebauung ergeben.

who consciously and deliberately combine monastic community life with pastoral and missionary service, building communities both within and outside the abbey.

The new oblong building closes the gap on the third side of a courtyard garden which was previously enclosed only on two sides. With it, a self-confident and new contemporary quality has been added to the heterogeneous buildings in the neighborhood. The new building adopts the principle of employing columns to line the corridor areas, as is the case with the medieval wing and the extension designed by Hans Schilling. The irregular geometry of the white-plastered new building appears folded. The folds allow the building to subtly react to the urban developmental and geometrical guidelines that are derived from the shape

Die Räume des Neubaus entsprechen ganz den Vorgaben des gemeinschaftlichen Klosterlebens, das neben gemeinsamen Mahlzeiten im Refektorium und dem Chorgebet in der Klosterkirche nach Orten und Räumen der Begegnung und Kommunikation verlangt, ebenso der Stille und Anbetung. Die Prämonstratenser verbinden dieses innere Leben der Klostergemeinschaft mit der nach außen gerichteten Seelsorge. Das zeigt sich auch in Hamborn: Direkt nebenan befinden sich das Abtei-Gymnasium, das Abteizentrum für Seminare und Tagungen, das St.-Johannes-Hospital und der Abteifriedhof, eingebettet mitten in die uralte Klosterpfarrei St. Johann und die umgebenden Pfarreien, allesamt Einsatzorte der Chorherren.

Das neue Gebäude bietet neben dem Wohntrakt einen Sakralraum, Büros und einen Rekreationsraum mit großen Türen zum Garten, Gesprächs- und Gruppenräume, Terrassen und einen Innenhof (Patio). Die unterschiedlichen Funktionen finden alle Platz unter einem gemeinsamen Dach. Organisiert sind die Räume entlang von liturgischen Wegen, die jeweils architektonisch umgesetzt

the shape of the site and the connecting heights of the existing buildings surrounding it.

The spaces inside the new building satisfy all the requirements of monastic community life which includes joint meals in the refectory and choral prayers in the monastery church, requiring places and spaces to meet and communicate, as well as those for silence and worship. The Premonstratensians combine the inner life of the monastic community with outwardly directed pastoral care. This is also evident in Hamborn: just next door is the abbey high school, the abbey center for seminars and conferences, St. John's Hospital, and the abbey cemetery which are all imbedded in the old vicarage of St. Johann and the neighboring vicarages that are also performance venues of the canons.

Apart from the residential wing, the new building provides a sacral chamber, offices and a recreation room with large doors that give onto the garden, the conversation and group spaces, terraces, and the patio. The different functions are all housed under one common roof while the spaces are organized around liturgical paths, each

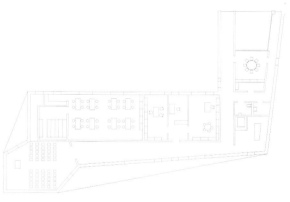

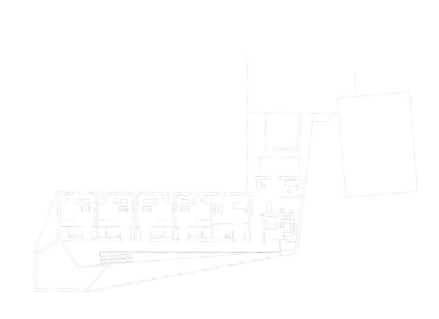

wurden: Im Erdgeschoss ist es zunächst eine historische Kreuzigungsgruppe, die optisch die Aufmerksamkeit in den Erweiterungsbau lenkt: erst den Blick und dann die Bewegung. Der Weg, von dem Gebäudebestand herkommend, führt vom romanischen Kreuzgang und damit von der Klosterkirche hin zur Kapelle am schmalen Ende des Riegels. Dieser kleine, vertikal aufstrebende Sakralraum mit Empore ist nach Osten orientiert, sodass beim Frühgebet Morgenlicht in den Raum fällt. Der Verbindung von Innen- und Außenleben folgend, hat er drei Zugänge: vom Inneren des Klosters her, vom Friedhof her und von der Straße bzw. der benachbarten Schule. Er kann zum Beispiel auch zur Aussegnung genutzt werden, für Gruppengottesdienste mit Schulklassen oder bei Einkehrtagen. So ist jetzt die gesamte Klosteranlage zwischen zwei sakralen Räumen gelegen, die durch die Kreuzgänge miteinander und mit dem Kloster verbunden sind.

Die beiden Obergeschosse sind privater. Hier sind entlang eines zweigeschossigen inneren Laubengangs die Kemenaten angeordnet. Eine goldene Stirnwand dient als optischer Kulminationspunkt der dynamischen diagonalen Flächen, die den Raum beschreiben.

Während der Neubau auf der Gartenseite die Stützenreihe des Nachbargebäudes weiterführt, setzt er sich zur Straßenseite mit seinen weißen Putzfassaden vom rotbraunen Klinker des Nachbarn dezidiert ab. Der Neubau hat ein flaches Pultdach und ist innen wie außen in warmem Altweiß gehalten, das an das Ordensgewand der Prämonstratenser erinnert. Kontrastiert werden die weißen Flächen mit Eichentüren und -böden, gestrichenem Beton und der Metall- und Glasfassade der Eingangsseite.

Der Erweiterungsbau ist hell und von Licht durchflutet – ein Hinweis darauf, dass „die Prämonstratenser sich dem Zeugnis für das Leben verpflichtet wissen", wie Abt Albert es formuliert: In all ihrem Tun bejahen sie das Leben, das der auferstandene Christus der Dunkelheit des Todes entgegenstellt.

with their own distinct architecture: on the first floor, an historical crucifixion group visually leads on to the extension building, guiding the eye and subsequent movement in space. Coming from the existing buildings, the path leads from the Romanesque cloister (and from the monastery church) to the chapel at the narrow end of the oblong building. This small, vertically rising sacral space, equipped with its own gallery, faces the east, permitting morning light during the early morning prayers. In keeping with the premise of intimately linking inside and outside, the chapel can be accessed from three sides: from the inside of the monastery, from the cemetery and from the street or the neighboring school. It can also be used for funeral services, for group services with school classes or for days of retreat. As such, the entire monastery complex is positioned between two sacral spaces that are connected with each other and to the monastery by the cloisters.

The two upper floors are more private in nature. Here, the bowers are lined along a double-story inner pergola. A golden front wall serves as optical apex of the dynamically-shaped diagonal surfaces that describe the space.

While the new building continues the neighboring building's row of columns on the garden side, it presents a distinct and different look to the street side, with its white-plastered facades starkly contrasting the reddish brown brick of the neighboring building. The new building has a flat pent roof and is dipped in a warm antique white hue both on the inside and the outside, bringing to mind the color of the Premonstratensian order's robes. The white surfaces are complemented by oak doors and floors, coated concrete, and the metal and glass facade of the entrance side.

The extension building is brightly lit, being suffused by light, understood as symbol of "the Premonstratensians' commitment to the testimonial of life", as Abbot Albert puts it. In all their actions, they strive to affirm life which the resurrected Christ contrasts with the darkness of death.

STÄDTEBAU
URBAN DESIGN

Was ASTOC auszeichnet, ist die Fähigkeit, auf allen Maßstabsebenen, von ganz groß nach ganz klein, zu denken, zu entwerfen und zu bauen. Ihre Haltung zeigt sich konkret in den Projekten in unterschiedlichen Phasen. Im architektonischen Detail werden die Ergebnisse des planerischen Denkens sichtbar. Dennoch haben sich die Entwerfer von ASTOC neben dem professionellen auch ihren persönlichen Blick auf die gebaute Umwelt erhalten: „Wie jeder andere auch gehe ich durch einen neuen Stadtteil wie die HafenCity in Hamburg, die nach unseren Plänen entstanden ist, und betrachte kritisch die Ergebnisse", erklärt Markus Neppl beispielsweise im Gespräch. ASTOCs städtebauliche Pläne zielen auf Vielfalt ab. Wenn die städtebaulichen Vorgaben so robust sind, dass auch mal ein nur zweitklassiger architektonischer Entwurf möglich ist, ohne dem Konzept seine Stärke zu nehmen, war ASTOCs Arbeit erfolgreich. Der städtebauliche Plan soll schließlich die einzelnen Gebäude überleben und der Austausch einzelner Elemente möglich sein. „Ein guter Masterplan erträgt auch vielfältige Architektur" – auf diese einfache Formel bringt es ASTOC.

Sich trotz einer über die Jahre gewachsenen Erfahrung und Professionalität eine Naivität im Sinne von Neugierde und Experimentierfreudigkeit zu erhalten, ist den Entwerfern bei ASTOC wichtig, denn diese Art von Unvoreingenommenheit hat Kraft und Charme. Ein Weg, die Herangehensweise an neue Projekte „frisch" zu halten, ist die Büro- und Projektstruktur bei ASTOC, die von den Partnern als „zwar bisweilen anstrengend, aber immer förderlich" beschrieben wird. Ein Schlüssel zu erfolgreichem Städtebau ist schließlich die Prozessgestaltung und die setzt im eigenen Haus an.

Beispiel HafenCity

Die Hamburger HafenCity ist das derzeit größte innerstädtische Stadtentwicklungsprojekt Europas. Der neue Stadtteil ist vollständig von Fluss- und Kanalläufen umgeben und hat eine Gesamtfläche von rund 150 Hektar. Bis Mitte der 2020er Jahre sollen hier Wohnraum für 12.000 Menschen und rund 40.000 Arbeitsplätze entstehen.

Anfang der 1990er Jahre zeigte sich, dass die damals knapp 100 Jahre alten Hafenbecken ungeeignet für die modernen Großschiffe wurden. Der Containerumschlag wurde zum Alten Elbtunnel verlagert. Die Erweiterung der Hafenanlagen konzentrierte sich auf den Ausbau der Kapazitäten im Westen. Durch die innenstadtnahe Lage der brachen Flächen bot sich eine einmalige Chance für die Stadtentwicklung. Nach einem städtebaulichen Wettbewerb wurde im Jahr 2000 mit dem Masterplan das Entwicklungskonzept für die Umwandlung des Hafenrandes zu einer Erweiterung der Hamburger Innenstadt veröffentlicht. Die insgesamt elf Quartiere des ursprünglichen Masterplans werden sukzessive von Westen nach Osten und von Norden nach Süden verwirklicht.

„Am Sandtorkai" ist das erste realisierte Quartier, bestehend aus fünf Wohn- und drei Bürogebäuden, mit Traditionsschiffhafen und einer Promenade unterhalb der überkragenden Gebäude. Mit dem Kaiserkai wurde auf der Landzunge zwischen dem Sandtorhafen und dem Grasbrookhafen das zweite Teilquartier errichtet. Zu den Besonderheiten dieses Quartiers gehören seine urbane Dichte, eine Vielfalt der Architekturen, die Promenaden und am Wasser gelegene Plätze sowie die Elbphilharmonie im Kaispeicher.

What distinguishes ASTOC from many other architecture and urban planning firms is their capacity to think, design and construct in many different scales, from the very large to the very small. The various phases that their projects run through wonderfully exemplify their unique approach. It is in the architectural detailing that the results of their planning approach become clearly visible, while the designers at ASTOC have always endeavored to add a personal touch to the built environment they create. "Like everyone else, I walk through a new urban district such as the HafenCity in Hamburg which we have planned, and critically examine the results", says Markus Neppl.

ASTOC's urban plans strive to create diversity. The firm views it as a measure of their success if their concepts, set within robust urban planning guidelines, are so resilient that they can tolerate even second-class architectural designs. After all, urban plans ought to be versatile enough to transcend the plane of individual buildings, enabling a rethink and renovation of individual elements. "A good master-plan should be able to stomach highly diverse architecture", says ASTOC succinctly.

It is important for ASTOC's designers to retain a sense of curiosity and experimentation, in spite of their long-standing experience and professional know-how, since these qualities bring new power and charm to the projects. A major contributing factor for ASTOC's "fresh" project approaches is its office and project implementation structure, described by the firm's partners as being "exhausting at times, but always fruitful". One of the keys to their successful urban planning is, last but not least, the constitution of the firm's internal working processes.

The HafenCity Example

Hamburg's HafenCity currently represents Europe's largest inner-city development project. The new urban district, with a total area of around 150 hectares, is surrounded by river and canal channels on all sides. By the middle of the twenty-twenties, it is envisaged to provide new residential space for up to 12,000 people, as well as create 40,000 new jobs.

At the beginning of the nineteen-nineties, it became clear that the docks, then almost 100 years old, were unsuitable for handling large, modern ships. As a result, the container terminal was relocated to the Old Elbe Tunnel. Extension of port facilities focused on increasing capacity in the western part of the city. The newly defunct area's prime inner-city location meant that a unique opportunity for new urban planning had opened up. Following an urban master-planning competition, the development concept together with the master-plan for the conversion of the edge of the port district and extension of the inner city of Hamburg to this location was published in 2000. A total of eleven district sectors as outlined in the original master-plan are to be successively realized from west to east and from north to south.

The Sandtorkai is the first district to be realized, consisting of five residential and three office buildings, the Tall Ship Harbor and a promenade below the cantilevered buildings. The Kaiserkai is the second realized district sector, located on the headland between the Sandtorhafen and the Grasbrookhafen. What makes this district sector special is its urban density, diverse architecture, the promenades and squares by the water, as well as the Elbphilharmonie at the Kaispeicher.

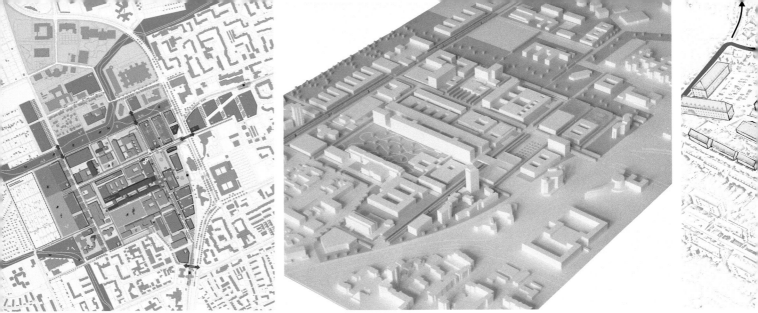

MASTERPLAN MEDIZINISCHE HOCHSCHULE HANNOVER MASTER-PLAN OF HANOVER MEDICAL SCHOOL

Am Ende des Sandtorhafenbeckens befindet sich das Quartier „Am Sandtorpark/Grasbrook". Dieses wird durch eine Nutzungsmischung von großen Bürohäusern, Wohngebäuden und einer Schule rund um den grünen Sandtorpark geprägt.

Das benachbarte Überseequartier am Magdeburger Hafen wird entlang des Überseeboulevards entwickelt, der das Viertel in seiner gesamten Länge von Norden nach Süden durchzieht. In den 14 Bauten am Boulevard liegen Einzelhandel und Gastronomie in den Erd- und ersten Obergeschossen. Der nördliche Teil wird durch Wohnungen, der südliche Teil durch Büros geprägt. Das Kreuzfahrtterminal mit Hotel, die Waterfront Towers und ein Science Center gehören ebenso zu den Magneten dieses Viertels wie die neue U-Bahn-Linie U4.

Die HafenCity wird ein lebendiges Stadtviertel mit Wohnungen, Geschäften, Parks und Promenaden, Büros, Kindergärten, Freizeit- und Tourismuseinrichtungen. Der Entwurf des Teams ASTOC/ Kees Christiaanse/Hamburgplan überzeugt durch seine große Bandbreite von städtebaulichen Typologien, die unterschiedliche Quartiere entstehen lassen und eine schrittweise Realisierung zulassen. Die Öffnung der HafenCity zur Speicherstadt ermöglicht eine gute Verzahnung von alter und neuer Stadt und bietet attraktive, neue Wohnlagen an den Hafenbecken und an der Elbe. Bei ASTOC glaubt man daran, dass eine gute Verfahrensbegleitung mehr bringt als ein „Handbuch für Gestaltung". Die architektonische Kenntnis erlaubt es, die Folgen der städtebaulichen Setzungen für die Architektur zu antizipieren und vorteilhaft zu gestalten. Der wichtigste Rahmen für die spätere Bebauung ist zunächst die Erschließung. Und hierfür sieht der Entwurf etwas Besonderes vor: Im Entwurf wurden die Elb-parallelen Strukturen um 90 Grad gedreht. Der Mittelteil, das Überseequartier, wird dadurch nicht zur Fortführung der Speicherstadt, sondern öffnet die HafenCity zur Elbe und zur Innenstadt. Das Überseequartier ist als Zentrum der Hafencity gedacht, in dem sich der Einzelhandel konzentriert und der mit dem Magdeburger Hafen einen Ort mit großer städtebaulicher Strahlkraft hat, der es sogar mit der Binnenalster aufnehmen kann.

Um eigenständige Quartiere herauszubilden, wurden die städtebaulichen Magnete nicht im Zentrum versammelt, sondern – in einem äußeren und einem inneren Dreieck – als präzise platzierte Gebäude an Orten, die mit besonderen Nutzungen auf die verschiedenen Viertel wirken können.

Kritiker bemängeln an der HafenCity, dass sie sich hauptsächlich an besserverdiende Mieter und Käufer wendet. Ist die Hafen-City vielleicht dabei, Opfer ihres eigenen Erfolgs zu werden? Die heutigen Preise übersteigen teilweise dramatisch die Herstellungskosten, sodass Hoffnung besteht, dass die derzeit „überzogenen Immobilienpreise wieder fallen, wenn der Hype vorbei ist", wie Markus Neppl es formuliert. Das schmerzt besonders angesichts der Tatsache, dass die Eigenheim- und die Sozialbauförderung abgeschafft wurden. Die Stadt Hamburg entschied sich daher zum Beispiel Baugruppen speziell zu unterstützen, um diesem Trend entgegenzuwirken. Weiterhin werden in den neuen östlichen Quartieren mehr Mietwohnungen angeboten und die Stadt Hamburg geht von ihrer Forderung, Höchstpreise für die Grundstücke zu erzielen, ab.

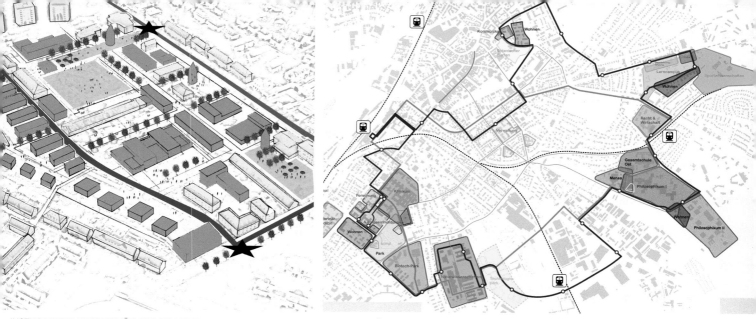

JUSTUS-LIEBIG-UNIVERSITÄT GIESSEN, TESTPLANUNGSVERFAHREN ZUR BAULICH-RÄUMLICHEN ENTWICKLUNG DER JUSTUS-LIEBIG-UNIVERSITÄT JUSTUS LIEBIG UNIVERSITY GIESSEN, TEST-PLANNING PROCESS FOR BUILDING DEVELOPMENT AT JUSTUS LIEBIG UNIVERSITY

At the end of the Sandtor dock, lies the district sector of Am Sandtorpark/Grasbrook which is characterized by mixed-use developments that include large office buildings, residential buildings and a school, all grouped around leafy Sandtorpark.

The neighboring overseas district sector at the Magdeburg Port is being developed along the overseas boulevard which traverses the entire length of the sector from north to south. The fourteen buildings lining the boulevard house retail businesses and restaurants, both on the first and second floors. The northern part is dedicated to apartments, the southern part to offices. A cruise terminal, a hotel, the Waterfront Towers, the Science Center, and the new metro line U4 are some of the main attractions of this sector.

The HafenCity is becoming a lively urban quarter with apartments, shops, parks, promenades, offices, nursery schools, and recreational as well as tourism facilities. The design of the team comprising ASTOC, Kees Christiaanse, and Hamburgplan, impresses on account of its wide range of urban planning typologies, permitting diverse urban quarters and a phased implementation. The HafenCity opens up towards the Speicherstadt, allowing for excellent interlinkages between the old and the new city, and offering attractive new living spaces by the inner harbor and the Elbe River. ASTOC firmly believes that good procedural support has more benefits to offer than the conventional practice of simply adhering to a "design manual". Architectural knowledge enables us to anticipate and positively shape the consequences of urban planning interventions for the architecture that they involve. The first and most important factor for gauging potential future building activity is the question

of access. This is where design comes in: in the said project, it has turned the structures that ran parallel to the Elbe River by ninety degrees. The middle part, the overseas quarter, hence does not become a continuation of the Speicherstadt, but opens up the HafenCity towards the Elbe River and the inner city. The overseas quarter has been envisaged as new center of the HafenCity where retail business is focused and which has great urban charisma due to the nearby Magdeburg Port, almost placing it in direct competition with the sophisticated Binnenalster.

In order to create discretely independent urban quarters, the urban magnets were not located around the center but in an outer and inner triangle, precisely placing buildings that would be able to shape the different quarters with their dedicated functions.

Critics have remarked that the HafenCity caters mainly to higher income tenants and property buyers. So the question may be asked whether the HafenCity is becoming a victim of its own success. Today's rates have, in parts, dramatically exceeded production costs which gives rise to the hope that the present "exorbitantly high real estate rates will fall again when the hype is over", as Markus Neppl puts it. For the current period, however, this is especially painful considering the fact that home ownership and social housing subsidies have been scrapped. What may come as a consolation to some, the city of Hamburg decided to provide special support to building groups, for instance, to counter this trend. Rented apartments continue to prevail in the new eastern quarters and the city of Hamburg has started to rethink its policy of constantly fetching maximum prices for the plots, in certain

KENNEDY BUSINESS CENTER, EINDHOVEN: ASTOC IN ZUSAMMENARBEIT MIT KCAP ARCHITECTS & PLANNERS, ROTTERDAM KENNEDY BUSINESS CENTER, EINDHOVEN: ASTOC IN COLLABORATION WITH KCAP ARCHITECTS & PLANNERS, ROTTERDAM

Ökologische Aspekte werden heute bisweilen stärker gefordert als ökonomische.

Die Hamburger Innenstadt liegt an der Alster. Die HafenCity hat das Potenzial, das Zentrum zu erweitern und die Innenstadt mit der Elbe zu verbinden. „Die ökonomischen und auch architektonischen Tendenzen führen in unserer heutigen Gesellschaft zu einer Fragmentierung, die wilde Patchwork-Neustädte hervorbringen kann" (Neppl). Städtebau hat deshalb die vordringlichste Aufgabe, über eine Ansammlung geballter Egoismen hinauszugehen und ein nachhaltiges, kohärentes Bild zu entwerfen und zu entwickeln, das dennoch nicht zum Korsett wird.

Beispiel Heidestraße in Berlin

Für das Areal am Hauptbahnhof in Berlin wurde ein städtebaulicher Wettbewerb veranstaltet, aus dem ASTOC als Sieger hervorging. Ihr Entwurf für das Gelände zwischen Invalidenstraße, Perleberger Brücke, Fernbahntrasse und Spandauer Schifffahrtskanal sieht die Anlage eines Stadthafens vor. Um ihn herum soll ein großstädtisches Quartier gebaut werden mit Kunstcampus, Marina, Restaurants, Wohnungen und Büros. Das innerstädtische Areal liegt an einem der wichtigsten europäischen Verkehrsknotenpunkte. Trotz einer städtischen Dichte sieht der Entwurf viel öffentlichen Raum vor und einen bis zu 30 Meter breiten, unbebauten Uferstreifen als öffentliche Promenade. Die Wohnhäuser mit circa 1200 Wohnungen folgen der Berliner Traufhöhe. Höhere Gebäude gibt es in den Büroquartieren am Hamburger Bahnhof und am Nordhafen. Drei neue Brücken werden das Quartier besser an die Stadt anbinden. Entlang einer Bahntrasse sollen neue Gewerbebauten die Wohnhäuser vom Verkehrslärm abschirmen. Um dem Gelände seine besondere Atmosphäre nicht zu nehmen, sollen die alten Speditionshallen zu Galerien umgebaut werden. Die wichtigste Idee war es, einfach „ein Stück Berlin" zu entwerfen. Am Anfang stand daher die Frage, wie sich Stadt an dieser Stelle entwickeln kann. Das Quartier wird in Zukunft für Millionen von Gästen der erste Eindruck von Berlin sein und ist deshalb eine wichtige städtebauliche Visitenkarte der Hauptstadt. Der Moment der Ankunft in Berlin hat die Planer deshalb besonders beschäftigt. Ihr Ziel ist es nicht, eine „völlig cleane" Musterstadt zu etablieren (Neppl). Sie wollen eher ein Bahnhofsviertel entwerfen als eine „Europa-City". Das Quartier darf ruhig „normaler" als der nahe Potsdamer Platz sein, denn es bietet das Potenzial, sich zum Kunstviertel zu entwickeln. ASTOC begann mit dem Selbstverständnis der Stadt – und nicht nur dem Ort an sich. Berlin entdeckt derzeit seine Wasserlagen neu und das neue Hafenbecken wird ein Magnet des Viertels sein. Die autobahnähnliche Situation der Heidestraße wollen die Architekten dringend aufbrechen und einen „klaren und präzisen Stadtraum" rund um den Hafen schaffen, der auch von der östlichen Promenade entlang des Schiffahrtskanals zur Wirkung kommen soll. Anders als bei der HafenCity in Hamburg wird bei diesem Berliner Beispiel die Planung fast nur von den nicht-städtischen Grundstückseigentümern bestimmt. Der Entwurf muss darauf achten, dass der Zusammenhang nicht verloren geht.

MASTERPLAN EUROPACITY BERLIN, RAHMENPLAN MASTER-PLAN FOR THE EUROPACITY BERLIN, PLANNING FRAMEWORK | MASTERPLAN EUROPACITY BERLIN
MASTER-PLAN EUROPACITY BERLIN

cases allowing ecological aspects to have a more urgent say than economic ones.

Hamburg's inner city lies on the banks of the Alster River. The HafenCity has the potential to extend the city center and to connect the inner city with the Elbe River." The economic as well as architectural tendencies in today's society lead to fragmentation, resulting in wild new patchwork cities", says Neppl. Therefore, urban development's most urgent task would be to transcend all the egoisms that exist, and to design and develop a sustainable and coherent vision which, for all its positive qualities, avoids the folly of becoming a stale corset.

The Example of Heidestrasse in Berlin

ASTOC won a master-plan competition for a site close to Berlin's central station. Their design envisages a town harbor on the site which is located between Invalidenstrasse, Perleberger Bridge, mainline railway tracks, and the Spandauer navigation channel. Planned to become the focus of a new metropolitan quarter, it will house an art campus, a marina, restaurants, apartments, and offices. The inner-city site lies close to one of Europe's most important traffic hubs. In spite of achieving metropolitan densities, the design offers plenty of public space and an inviting riverside promenade up to thirty meters wide. The residential buildings accommodating around 1,200 apartments adhere to the city's eaves height.

Buildings of greater height are located in the office quarters at the Hamburger Bahnhof and the Nordhafen. Three new bridges will improve connectivity to the city. Along a railway line, new commercial buildings are to shield the residential buildings from traffic noise. In order to preserve the site's special atmosphere, the old shipping company halls are to be converted to galleries. The general idea was to design "a piece of Berlin." As such, the question initially was to find out how the city can develop at this particular location. The urban quarter will, in future, be Berlin's first impression for millions of visitors. It is therefore an important urban "visiting card" for the capital. The moment of arrival in Berlin occupied the minds of the planners in particular. It was not their goal to produce "a totally sterilized" model city, as Neppl has said. Rather, it was their intention to design a station district, instead of a type of "city of Europe." The district was allowed to be somewhat more "normal" than the high-strung Potsdamer Platz in the vicinity, holding out the potential to develop into a more laid back art district. ASTOC's approach was based on the self-image of the city as a whole and not just on the location itself. Berlin is currently rediscovering its waterfronts. The new town harbor will become a magnet of the quarter. The architects want to promptly redesign the highway-like Heidestrasse, intending to create a "clear and precise urban space" all around the harbor which may also be experienced from the eastern promenade along the navigation canal. In contrast to the HafenCity in Hamburg, the planning in this example from Berlin is almost entirely determined by non-urban plot owners. The design has to take care not to lose sight of the inherent contexts.

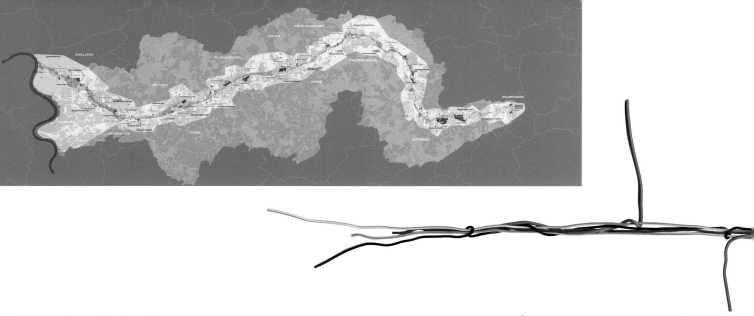

MASTERPLAN EMSCHER ZUKUNFT MASTER-PLAN EMSCHER ZUKUNFT | FARBIGER KABELSTRANG ALS SYMBOL FÜR DIE „NEUE EMSCHER" COLORFUL CABLE HARNESS AS SYMBOL FOR THE "NEW EMSCHER"

Beispiel Masterplan Emscher-Zukunft

Ein gutes Beispiel für das Planen im größeren Maßstab bei ASTOC ist der Masterplan für die Emscher: ein 85 Kilometer langer Flusslauf mit einer Fläche von circa 4000 Hektar! Während der Industrialisierung des Ruhrgebiets wurde die Emscher zum Kanal für industrielle Abwässer. Das Städteband des Ruhrgebiets wandte sich von seinem unattraktiv gewordenen Strom ab. Zur planenden ARGE gehören auch RMP Landschaftsarchitekten, Landschaft Planen und Bauen sowie Post und Welters. Der Entwurf einer langfristigen Strategie, Planungsmethodik und Prozessgestaltung wurde von ASTOC erarbeitet. Nach geltendem EU-Recht ist es heute nicht mehr möglich, Abwässer ungeklärt oberflächlich zu kanalisieren. Der Masterplan sieht vor, die Emscher wieder zu einem attraktiven Fluss zu machen. Wegen des Geruchs blieb traditionell ein 200 bis 300 Meter breiter Streifen um den Fluss herum unbebaut. Heute werden neue Klärwerke gebaut, die Wasserqualität steigt und die Emscher kann erstmals wieder ein zusammenhängender Raum werden, der quer durch das nördliche Ruhrgebiet führt. Die Anrainer-Städte können sich erstmals wieder zu ihrem Fluss hinwenden. Die Emschergenossenschaft wurde 1899 als erster deutscher Wasserwirtschaftsverband gegründet und nimmt sich des Umbaus der Flusslandschaft und der Renaturierung des Gewässers an. Das Projekt besteht aus einer umfassenden Regionalplanung mit starkem Kommunikationsanteil. Der große Blickwinkel hilft, die Qualitäten, die durch das Projekt möglich werden, klar zu sehen. Ein durchgehender Radweg entlang der Emscher ist nur ein kleines Beispiel für die neuen Nutzungen. Die Bilder und Pläne von ASTOC helfen bei der Kommunikation des langwierigen Projektes, dessen Realisierung sich über Jahre erstreckt und dessen Erfolge erst in 20 Jahren voll sichtbar werden.

Beispiel Campusentwicklung

Nicht erst mit dem Wettbewerbserfolg für die Planung und Realisierung der neuen „Hochschule Ruhr West" in Mülheim an der Ruhr 2010 richtet sich der Blick von ASTOC verstärkt auch auf Campus-Planungen für verschiedene Universitäten und Krankenhäuser. Der Entwurf der Arbeitsgemeinschaft ASTOC/HPP Architekten für den neuen Hochschulcampus in Mülheim ging als Sieger aus einem zweistufigen Wettbewerb mit 16 Teilnehmern hervor. Der Campus zeigt sich als städtebaulich integriertes Ensemble mit acht differenzierten Baukörpern, vier Institutsgebäuden, drei Sonderbauten (Hörsaalzentrum, Mensa und Bibliothek) und einem Parkhaus. Im Mittelpunkt des Entwurfs stehen das Thema Einheit und Vielfalt bei der Fassadengestaltung der Baukörper, die das Erscheinungsbild des Campus prägen wird, sowie die Gestaltung der öffentlichen Räume zur Aufwertung und Belebung des angrenzenden Stadtgebiets. Die nachhaltige Gebäudekonzeption und das technische Versorgungskonzept bringen minimierten Bedarf an Energie und Ressourcen mit einem hohen Nutzerkomfort in Einklang. Mit den Bauarbeiten soll im Frühjahr 2012 begonnen werden, die Fertigstellung ist für 2014 vorgesehen. Der Hochschulbau in Deutschland entwickelt sich derzeit weg von der traditionellen „Bedarfsplanung", die den Städten kaum Raum für Engagement ließen. Mit der zunehmenden Konkurrenz unter den Hochschulen genügt auch bau-

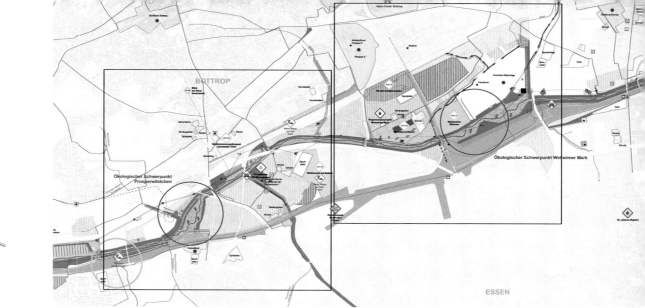

The Example of the Master-Plan Emscher-Zukunft

A good example for ASTOC's large-scale planning is the master-plan for the Emscher River, consisting of an 85 kilometer long river with an area as large as around 4,000 hectares. During the industrialization of the Ruhr region, the Emscher River was transformed into a canal for industrial effluents. The ring of cities of the Ruhr region turned its back on the river that had become unattractive. The appointed planning firm ARGE works together with RMP Landscape Architects, Landschaft Planen und Bauen, and Post und Welters. ASTOC delivered a design for a long-term strategy, planning methodology and process management. According to current EU law, it is not anymore permissible today, to channel untreated effluents into open rivers. The master-plan intends to turn the Emscher River into an attractive river again. Due to the smell, a 200 to 300 meter wide strip around the river has habitually always remained free of built structures. Today, new wastewater treatment plants are being built, the water quality is improving and the Emscher River can, for the first time, again become an integrated and coherent space running across the northern Ruhr region. The neighboring cities can, for the first time, again turn to their river. The Emscher Cooperative, founded in 1899, was the first German water industry association and has taken on the challenge of transforming the river landscape and re-naturalizing the body of water. The project consists of comprehensive regional planning interventions with a strong emphasis on communication. The wide view taken helps to clearly see the qualities that the project makes possible. A continuous cycle track along the Emscher River represents only a glimpse of the many new uses that are possible. ASTOC's images and plans support communication processes of this lengthy project whose realization is spread over many years and whose success will only be clearly seen in twenty years.

The Example of Campus Development

As ASTOC's 2010 competition success for the planning and realization of the new building at Ruhr West University of Applied Sciences in Mülheim exemplifies, the firm continues to be engaged in planning campuses for various universities as well as hospitals. The design, jointly submitted by ASTOC and HPP Architects for the new university campus in Mülheim, was awarded first prize in a two-stage competition that involved sixteen participants. The campus is envisaged to become an ensemble that is integrated into the town, with eight distinctive buildings, four institutional buildings, three special purpose buildings (including the lecture hall center, the canteen and the library), as well as a parking facility. The design focuses on creating unity as well as diversity in terms of the facade design of the buildings which will shape the look of the campus, and in terms of the design of the public spaces, upgrading and reinvigorating the neighboring urban area. The sustainable building concept as well as the technical services concept, harmonizes minimal energy and resource use with a high degree of user comfort. Construction is slated to begin in spring 2012, with completion envisaged for 2014. University campus planning in Germany is currently moving away from the conventional concept of "requirement planning" which doesn't leave much maneuvering space for

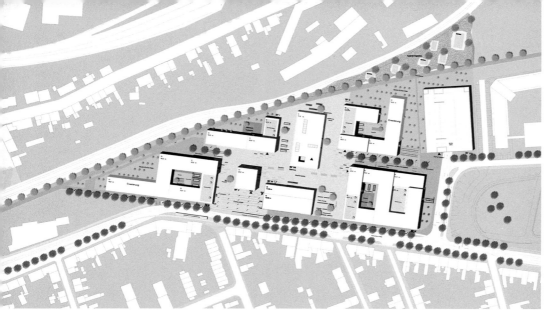

NEUBAU DER HOCHSCHULE RUHR-WEST, MÜLHEIM AN DER RUHR NEW BUILDING OF THE RUHR-WEST UNIVERSITY OF APPLIED SCIENCES, MÜLHEIM AN DER RUHR

lich der „niedrigste gemeinsame Nenner" nicht mehr. Universitäten sollen und wollen baulich wieder stärker in der Stadt präsent sein und genießen ihre architektonische Ausstrahlung. Um bessere Stadtbausteine zu werden, müssen auch Hochschulbauten attraktive Erdgeschosse bekommen und ansprechende städtische Räume bilden. Angenehme Eingangs- und Aufenthaltsbereiche gehören ebenso dazu. Wenn es bereits Bestandsgebäude auf dem Campus gibt, nutzt ASTOC die Erweiterung gerne, um den Bestand mit den Neubauten zu verknüpfen.

ASTOC hat sich mit der Planung von Klinik-Campussen bereits mehrfach beschäftigt und beispielsweise für Spitäler in Zürich und Bern und die Medizinische Hochschule Hannover städtebauliche Fragestellungen untersucht. Einige Planungsprinzipien finden sich auch in Hochschulplanungen wie denen für die ETH Zürich, die Universitäten Köln, Gießen, Göttingen, Kassel, Tübingen und Paderborn.

Beispiel Neue Düsseldorfer Stadtquartiere

Das Areal der Neuen Düsseldorfer Stadtquartiere liegt zentrumsnah im Stadtteil Derendorf. Nach einem Workshop-Verfahren im Jahr 2000 hat sich das Projekt außerordentlich zielgerichtet und kontinuierlich entwickelt.

Das schmale „krawattenförmige" Areal wird durch alternierende Bebauungsbänder in mehrere Baufelder gegliedert. So entsteht Raum für unterschiedliche öffentliche Freiräume, die sogenannten „Stadtgärten". Die baulich-räumliche Struktur orientiert sich an der Bebauung der benachbarten Gründerzeitviertel, ist gegliedert in

unterschiedliche Dichten und besitzt eine Hochhaussilhouette im südlichen Bereich. Das multifunktionale Nutzungskonzept bietet die Voraussetzungen für ein urbanes und lebendiges Stadtquartier.

Um dem Lärmschutz zu genügen, wurde die Erschließungsstraße in die Nachbarschaft der Bahntrasse nach außen gelegt. Die Hälfte der Flächen bleibt unbebaut. Ein wichtiger Teil des Konzepts war die Zwischennutzung für einige bestehende Bahnhallen auf dem Gelände, die – als „Les Halles" tituliert – als Katalysator der Entwicklung dienten. Niedrige Mieten machten in den Hallen Nutzungen möglich, die das Areal im öffentlichen Bewusstsein verankerten und einen positiven Standorteffekt hatten.

Entgegen der ursprünglichen Einschätzung fanden die Wohnungen eine stärkere Abnahme als die Büros. Nach Meinung von ASTOC müssen städtebauliche Pläne es aushalten können, wenn das Interesse an einer Nutzung nachlässt, während es für eine andere wächst.

Forschungsprojekt „elektrisch mobil.owl" am Lehrstuhl für Stadtplanung und Städtebauliches Entwerfen der Detmolder Schule für Architektur und Innenarchitektur, Prof. Oliver Hall

Häufig verbindet sich die wissenschaftliche Expertise an der Hochschule mit der praktischen Arbeit des Büros, sichtbar an Forschungsprojekten, wie zum Beispiel „Elektromobilität und erneuerbare Energien im ländlichen Raum".

Hierbei geht es nicht um die technisch/wirtschaftliche Einführung der Elektromobilität, sondern vielmehr um eine ganzheitliche Sicht und ein Umdenken auf mehreren Ebenen: Mit dem aus EFRE Mit-

NEUE DÜSSELDORFER STADTQUARTIERE NEW URBAN QUARTERS IN DÜSSELDORF

cities. With increasing competition amongst universities, what is conventionally considered best building practice may not be good enough anymore. Universities ought to and would like to become more prominent in their respective cities and are beginning to cherish their architectural charisma. In order to turn into positive urban elements within the matrix of the city, university buildings too must have more attractive first floors and inviting public spaces. This also applies to entrances and meeting spaces. Moreover, ASTOC likes to use the opportunity of integrating existing buildings on a campus into new building plans, thereby establishing new links. ASTOC has gained crucial experience with the planning of hospital campuses in a variety of projects, investigating urban planning issues for hospitals in Zurich and Bern, and for the Hanover Medical School, for example. Some of these planning principles are also applied to university campus planning as in the projects for the ETH Zurich and the universities of Cologne, Giessen, Göttingen, Kassel, Tübingen, and Paderborn.

The Example of the Neue Düsseldorfer Stadtquartiere

The site of the Neue Düsseldorfer Stadtquartiere (New Urban Quarters of Düsseldorf) lies close to the city center in the district of Derendorf. Following a workshop in 2000, the project has very steadily and purposefully developed.

The narrow, necktie-shaped site is divided into several building areas by alternating building strips. This frees up space for various public and open spaces, known as the so-called Stadtgärten (city gardens). The spatial and built structure is guided by the buildings of the neighboring Wilhelminian period and is divided into different densities, with the silhouette of a high-rise building in the southern part. The multifunctional usage concept offers ideal conditions to create a lively urban quarter.

In order to satisfy noise protection guidelines, the access road was relocated to the outside, in close proximity to the railroad tracks. Half the area remains free of buildings. An important part of the concept was the interim usage for a few existing railroad sheds on the site, called "Les Halles", which serve as catalysts for the development. Low rents have enabled uses to flourish in the sheds that made the site part of public consciousness and had a positive effect on the location as a whole.

Contrary to initial expectations, the apartments sold better than the offices. According to ASTOC, urban development plans must be versatile enough to withstand the diminishment of certain uses and the increased prevalence of others.

Research Project "elektrisch mobil.owl" at the Chair for City Planning and Urban Design, Detmold School of Architecture and Interior Design, Professor Oliver Hall

University-based scientific expertise frequently links up with the practical work of the firm, becoming evident in research projects such as "Electric Mobility and Renewable Energy in Rural Areas".

This project is not concerned with the technical or techno-economic feasibility of electric mobility, but rather with more holistic views that involve a rethink on several levels: with his research project "elektrisch-mobil.owl", supported by EFRE funds, Professor Oliver

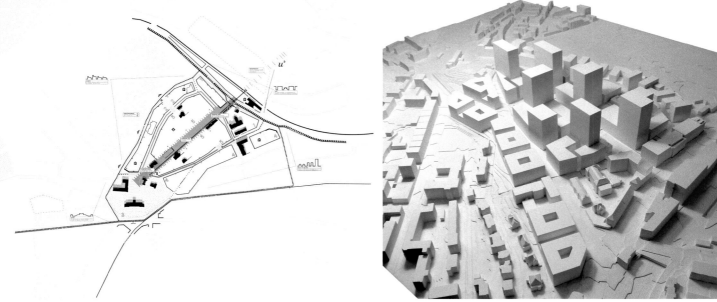

MASTERPLAN INSELSPITAL BERN (CH) MASTER-PLAN INSELSPITAL BERN (CH)

teln geförderten Forschungsprojekt „elektrisch-mobil.owl" sensibilisiert Prof. Oliver Hall an der Hochschule OWL für den ländlichen Raum, mit seinen kleinen und mittelgroßen Städten. Die Herausforderung aus planerischer Sicht ist dabei ein Gesamtkonzept nicht zum Produkt „Auto", sondern zur Dienstleistung „Mobilität" in all seinen Facetten bzgl. Nachhaltigkeit, Regional- und Stadtentwicklung und den kommunikativen Prozessen zwischen allen Beteiligten.

Kleine Städte und ländlicher Raum

Trotz der großen Erfolge, die ASTOC zum Beispiel bei den genannten Projekten in den Großstädten Berlin, Düsseldorf, München und Hamburg hat, interessieren sich die Architekten auch für die kleinen Städte und den ländlichen Raum, die schließlich die Lebenswirklichkeit der großen Mehrheit der Menschen in Deutschland sind. Sie beobachten dabei einen sanften Zwang zu einer neuen Arbeitsteilung zwischen den Kommunen, denn nicht jede Kommune kann alle sozialen, kulturellen oder Sporteinrichtungen haben. So bedarf es oft des Blicks von außen, um „die Wahrheiten aufzudecken, an Problemen, aber auch an Qualitäten", wie Oliver Hall es formuliert. Als externer Berater kann man die Stadt oft besser (er-)klären, und manchmal findet man dabei wahre „Goldschätze".

Planung bedeutet hier für ASTOC zum Beispiel vorhandene Ressourcen, wie Freiflächen, überschaubare Dimensionen und Entschleunigung, als Qualitäten aufzudecken.

„Planung schafft einen Raum, in dem die beteiligten Partner miteinander kommunizieren", formuliert Oliver Hall. Er begreift ASTOC als „Medium". Dieses Medium ist jedoch nicht dazu verdammt, lediglich passiv zu „sammeln". Eine aktive Masterplanung schafft einen wachsenden Konsens unter den Beteiligten, weil sich visuell klären lässt, was gewollt oder sinnvoll ist und was nicht. „Verbal, visuell, juristisch und ökonomisch gestalten wir unsere Planung so, dass sie ein ‚Ja' oder ‚Nein' verlangt", so Hall. Neppl pflichtet ihm bei, wenn er sagt, dass er Auftraggeber gerne mit der Aussage überrascht, dass er die Lösung selber (vorab) nicht kenne. Dies ist kein Ausdruck von Willfährigkeit, sondern im Gegenteil von einer gefestigten Ausgangsposition, die die relevanten Themen und Konflikte zunächst lokalisiert und damit keine reine Moderation ist. Der Planer muss dann „abwägen, begleiten und provozieren." Erst die Darstellung macht die Themen diskutabel und abwägbar und befähigt die Entscheider zur Entscheidung. Die Entwürfe zielen nicht auf eine architektonische Ikonensammlung. Gegensätze sind schließlich auch im Städtebau reizvoll und erst die Spannung führt zu Urbanität. So betrachtet, erfordert jeder neue Entwurf uneingeschränkte Neugierde und wird zur „Fitness-Aufgabe" für alle Akteure.

STRATEGISCHES STRASSEN- UND WEGEKONZEPT KREIS HÖXTER STRATEGIC ROAD AND TRACK CONCEPT FOR THE HÖXTER DISTRICT| ELEKTROMOBILITÄT UND ERNEUERBARE ENERGIEN IM LÄNDLICHEN RAUM ELECTRIC MOBILITY AND RENEWABLE ENERGY IN RURAL AREAS

Hall from OWL University devotes attention to rural areas with their small and medium-sized cities. From a planning perspective, the challenge is to develop an overall concept, not for the automobile as a commodity, but for the service of mobility in all its facets, involving sustainability, regional and urban development and the communicative processes taking place between all concerned.

Small Cities and Rural Areas

In spite of the impressive successes ASTOC has had, for example, with the above-stated projects in large cities such as Berlin, Düsseldorf, Munich and Hamburg, the architects are also interested in smaller cities and rural areas which constitute the living space of the majority of people living in Germany. What ASTOC have observed in the process is growing pressure to adopt a new distribution of tasks in the municipalities since not every municipality is able to offer all social, cultural or sporting infrastructures. Hence, a fresh view from afar is often beneficial "to find truths as relating to problems but also to qualities," as Oliver Hall has put it. External advisors can often explain the city better, and sometimes real "golden treasures" are discovered.

For ASTOC, this sort of planning means, for example, the definition of new qualities in terms of available resources such as open spaces, human scales, healthy moderation and deceleration.

"Planning creates a space in which the concerned partners can communicate with each other", says Oliver Hall. He sees ASTOC as a specific "medium". This medium is, however, not condemned to passively engage in the act of collecting. Active master-planning creates growing consensus among all participants as it can visually determine what is really required or purposeful and what is not. "In verbal, visual, legal, and economic terms, we devise our planning efforts in such a way as to demand a clear "yes" or "no" in the end", says Hall. Neppl agrees when he says that he likes to surprise clients by letting them know that even he himself does not know the required solutions beforehand. This is not an expression of submissiveness but, on the contrary, one of a consolidated starting position that allows relevant issues and conflicts to be localized first, thereby transcending its pure moderation role. In a second step, planners have to "assess, accompany and provoke." It is the presentation that is crucial for allowing issues to be debated and assessed, enabling the concerned persons to reach a decision. The designs do not intend to be an architectural icon collection of sorts. After all, contrasts are attractive in urban planning, creating the necessary suspense that is needed for urbanity to result. Seen in this light, every new design demands a sense of unrestricted curiosity, turning it into a measure of health for the entire design process and for all concerned.

V.L.N.R. F.L.T.R. PROF. OLIVER HALL [GESELLSCHAFTER ASSOCIATE] I INGO KANEHL [GESCHÄFTSFÜHRER CEO] I JÖRG ZIOLKOWSKI [GESCHÄFTSFÜHRER CEO] I PETER BERNER [GESCHÄFTSFÜHRENDER GESELLSCHAFTER MANAGING ASSOCIATE] I PROF. MARKUS NEPPL [GESELLSCHAFTER ASSOCIATE] I ANDREAS KÜHN [GESCHÄFTSFÜHRER CEO]

Peter Berner

Dipl.-Ing. Architekt BDA, geboren 1963 in Köln, studierte Architektur an der RWTH Aachen von 1983 bis 1990. 1989 erhielt er als Mitglied der studentischen Planungsgruppe Artecta den Schinkelpreis.

1990 gründete er zusammen mit Kees Christiaanse, Oliver Hall und Markus Neppl das Büro ASTOC Architects and Planners. Seit 2008 Mitglied im Gestaltungsbeirat der Stadt Köln, seit 2009 Mitglied im Landesvorstand des BDA NRW und seit 2011 Vorsitzender des Architektur Forum Rheinland e.V.

Ingo Kanehl

Dipl.-Ing. Architekt MBA, geboren 1971 in Minden, studierte Architektur von 1992 bis 1999 an der Hochschule Bochum und absolvierte von 2006 bis 2008 ein MBA-Studium an der Universität Duisburg-Essen/Zollverein School.

1999 arbeitete er bei Otto Steidle/Peter Schmitz Architekten in Köln. 2000 trat er in das Büro ASTOC Architects and Planners ein und ist seit 2009 Geschäftsführer. Lehraufträge für Baukonstruktion und Entwerfen an der RWTH Aachen (2000 bis 2001) und für Städtebau und Entwerfen an der Fachhochschule Köln (seit 2010).

Andreas Kühn

Dipl.-Ing. Architekt, geboren 1961 in Remscheid, studierte Architektur an der RWTH Aachen von 1983 bis 1990. 1989 erhielt er als Mitglied der studentischen Planungsgruppe Artecta den Schinkelpreis.

Tätigkeiten im Büro Prof. Jörg Friedrich, Hamburg (1990 bis 1991); als Projektleiter im Büro HPP Hentrich-Petschnigg und Partner, Hamburg (1991 bis 1995) und als Büroleiter im Büro von HPP, Dresden (1995 bis 1999) sowie als Projektleiter auf Bauherrenseite im Büro ABG Allgemeine Baubetreuungsgesellschaft, Köln (1999 bis 2002). 2003 trat er als Partner in das Büro ASTOC Architects and Planners ein und ist seit 2009 Geschäftsführer.

Peter Berner

Diploma in engineering/architecture BDA. Born in Cologne in 1963, he studied architecture at the RWTH Aachen from 1983 to 1990. As a member of the student planning group Artecta, he won the Schinkel Prize in 1989.

In 1990 he founded the office ASTOC Architects and Planners with Kees Christiaanse, Oliver Hall and Markus Neppl. He has been a member of Cologne City Planning Committee since 2008 and a board member of the BDA NRW since 2009. He became president of the Architektur Forum Rheinland e.V. in 2011.

Ingo Kanehl

Diploma in engineering/architecture MBA. Born in Minden in 1971, he studied architecture at the University of Bochum from 1992 to 1999; MBA degree at the University of Duisburg-Essen/Zollverein School from 2006 to 2008.

In 1999 he worked for Otto Steidle/Peter Schmitz Architects, Cologne. In 2000 he joined ASTOC Architects and Planners, where he has been a CEO since 2009. He has taught architectural construction and design at the RWTH Aachen (2000 to 2001), and urban development and planning at the Fachhochschule Cologne (since 2010).

Andreas Kühn

Diploma in engineering/architecture. Born in Remscheid in 1961, he studied architecture at the RWTH Aachen from 1983 to 1990. As a member of the student planning group Artecta, he won the Schinkel Prize in 1989.

Work in the office of Prof. Jörg Friedrich, Hamburg (1990 to 1991), as project head in the office HPP Hentrich-Petschnigg und Partner, Hamburg (1991 to 1995), and head of office at HPP, Dresden (1995 to 1999); also project head for building clients at ABG Allgemeine Baubetreuungsgesellschaft, Cologne (1999 to 2002). In 2003 he joined ASTOC Architects and Planners, where he has been a CEO since 2009.

Markus Neppl

Dipl.-Ing. Architekt BDA, geboren 1962 in Duisburg, studierte Architektur an der RWTH Aachen von 1983 bis 1990. 1989 erhielt er als Mitglied der studentischen Planungsgruppe Artecta den Schinkelpreis.

1990 gründete er zusammen mit Kees Christiaanse, Peter Berner und Oliver Hall das Büro ASTOC Architects and Planners. Lehraufträge an den Fachhochschulen in Bochum (1997) und Köln (1998). Professuren für Städtebau und Entwerfen an der Universität Kaiserslautern (1999 bis 2003) und für Stadtquartiersplanung und Entwerfen an der Technischen Hochschule in Karlsruhe (2003 bis heute). Seit 2008 ist er Dekan der Fakultät für Architektur am KIT Karlsruhe.

Markus Neppl

Diploma in engineering/architecture BDA. Born in Duisburg in 1962, he studied architecture at the RWTH Aachen from 1983 to 1990. As a member of the student planning group Artecta, he won the Schinkel Prize in 1989.

In 1990 he founded the office ASTOC Architects and Planners with Kees Christiaanse, Peter Berner and Oliver Hall. He has taught at polytechnics in Bochum (1997) and Cologne (1998). Professor of urban development and planning at the University of Kaiserslautern (1999 to 2003) and of local regional planning and design at the Technical University, Karlsruhe (2003 to now). He has been Dean of the Faculty of Architecture at the KIT Karlsruhe since 2008.

Oliver Hall

Dipl.-Ing. Architekt BDA, geboren 1962 in Köln, studierte Architektur an der RWTH Aachen von 1982 bis 1990. 1989 erhielt er als Mitglied der studentischen Planungsgruppe Artecta den Schinkelpreis. 1990 gründete er zusammen mit Kees Christiaanse, Peter Berner und Markus Neppl das Büro ASTOC Architects and Planners. Lehrauftrag für Städtebau und Entwerfen an der Fachhochschule Bochum (2002 bis 2003), seit 2003 Professur für Stadtplanung und städtebauliches Entwerfen an der Detmolder Schule für Architektur und Innenarchitektur (ein Fachbereich der Hochschule Ostwestfalen-Lippe).

Oliver Hall

Diploma in engineering/architecture BDA. Born in Cologne in 1962, he studied architecture at the RWTH Aachen from 1982 to 1990. As a member of the student planning group Artecta, he won the Schinkel Prize in 1989.

In 1990 he founded the office ASTOC Architects and Planners with Kees Christiaanse, Peter Berner and Markus Neppl. He taught urban development and planning at the Fachhochschule Bochum from 2002-3; since 2003 he has been professor of urban planning and design at Detmold School of Architecture and Interior Design (University of Ostwestfalen-Lippe).

Jörg Ziolkowski

Dipl.-Ing. Architekt, geboren 1964 in Karlsruhe, studierte Architektur an der RWTH Aachen von 1985 bis 1992.

Nach Tätigkeiten in den Büros von Jim Shay Architects, San Francisco (1992) und HPP Hentrich-Petschnigg und Partner, Hamburg und Düsseldorf (1992 bis 1994), Assistent am Lehrstuhl für Baukonstruktion und Entwerfen der RWTH Aachen (1994 bis 2001). 1995 gründete er das Büro Ziolkowski.WS Architektur mit Sitz in Köln. 2008 trat er in das Büro ASTOC Architects and Planners ein und ist seit 2009 Geschäftsführer.

Jörg Ziolkowski

Diploma in engineering/architecture. Born in Karlsruhe in 1964, studied architecture at the RWTH Aachen from 1985 to 1992.

After working in the offices of Jim Shay Architects, San Francisco (1992) and HPP Hentrich-Petschnigg und Partner, Hamburg and Düsseldorf (1992 to 1994), and as assistant to the Chair of Architectural Construction and Planning at the RWTH Aachen (1994 to 2001), he founded Ziolkowski.WS Architektur, Cologne in 1995. In 2008 he joined ASTOC Architects and Planners, where he has been a CEO since 2009.

DIE MITARBEITER 1991–2011
THE COLLABORATORS 1991–2011

Axel Albrecht, Alessandro Alivesi, Elisabeth Althoff, Norbert Althoff, Manuela Altmeyer, Timo Amann, Julia Anslinger, Sabine Arntz, Miren Aurtenetxe, Susanne Barth, Martina Baum, Hannah Becker, Ralf Bender, Martin Berchtold, Simon Berg, Mirko Bergmann, Peter Berner, Sophie Beuter, Zafer Bildir, Christina Blanck, Sebastian Blecher, Philipp Böddeker, Tim Bruckhoff, Ruth Bünker, Richard Büsching, Raphael Büsing, Kees Christiaanse, Charlie Deda, Silke Deffur, Anja Dick, Christian Dieckmann, Christoph Durban, Lisa Effing, Frank Eittorf, Felix Elbert, Oliver Ernst, Dirk Faltin, Daniel Festag, Niels Frerichmann, Judith Freund, Brian Freundt, Uwe Bernd Friedemann, Wolfram Georg, Marco de Giovannini, Stefanie Glausch, Christian Glöckner, Ute Goldbeck, Lars Goldstein, Agnieszka Gora, Sarah Gräfer, Cathrin Gramminger, Silke Grapenthin, Frank Grätz, Fabian Greiff, Eva Grimm, Johannes Groote, Florian Groß, Justine Grüner, Canan Güngör, Benjamin Günther, Fisun Gurpinar, Ann-Kathrin Habighorst, Oliver Hall, Denise Handler, Christian Hartmann, Nils Hartmann, Petra Hartmann, Manuel Hauer, Julia Hausmann, Dorothee Heidrich, Christian Herbert, Kerstin Herkenrath, Michael Herman, Sebastian Hermann, Lena Hocke, Till Hoevel, Karen Höfer, Jan Hogen, Till Hoinkis, Raul Hölzel, Sascha Hübel, Tom Huber, Rüdiger Hundsdörfer, Ulrich Hundsdörfer, Norman Jäckel, Samuel Jäger, Hendrik Jansen, Inga Joch, Rainer Johann, Ingo Kanehl, Daniela Kaufmann, Mirco Kaus, Markus Kersting, Simon Kettel, Tibor Kiss, Jan Klassen, Kirsten Kleine, Sabine Kovacs, Jacob Kramer, Philipp Krass, Fiona Kraus, Barbara Krehl, Nicolas Kretschmann, Stefanie Kufner, Andreas Kühn, Ralf Kunz, Dana Kurz, Till Kurz, Kathrin Kutter, Christoph Lajendäcker, Oliver Lambrecht, Markus Lang, Tobias Lechtenfeld, Dirk Lellau, Bettina Lelong, David Lemberski, Petra Lenschow, Ann Lüdecke, Jan Maassen, Maria Maennling, Henning Magirius, Christian Marquardt, Maria Mateos, Victoria Mateos, Alice Mathias, Ariane Mees, Marcel Mehler, Guido Meier, Uli Meier, Kristina Menken, Christian Meyer, Ludwig Meyer (†), Cathérine Minnameyer, Octavio Morales, Florian Morgen (†), Jan Müllender, Florian Müller, Claudia Mundt, Philip Mußler, Tanja Nelles, Markus Neppl, Emil Neumann, Valentin Niessen, Neda Nohadani, Maria Nome-Dahl, Anna Ohlmeier, Leo Oorschot, Beatrix Opolka, Tim Orth, Anne Osenberg, Sabine Paul, Philipp Pellio, Sebastian Perez-Prat, Miriam Pfeiffer, Norbert Philippen, Ute Pientka, Marcel Piethan, Michael Pique, Tobias Pretscher, Daniela Renner, Tim Rettler, Sabrina Rieger, Tim Rieniets, Markus Ritter, Diana Rogasch, Michael Rosemann, Martin Rößler, Sandra de Ruiz de Aluza, Gabriela Rusch, Tobias Rutkowski, Tycho Saariste, Thorsten Salmen, Michael Sandke, Magdalena Schaller, Jörg Schatzmann, Rawand Schika, Ansgar Schmidt, Oliver Schmidt, Katja Schmieder, Daniel Schnabel, Alexander Schnieber, Katja Schotte, Hermann Schratz, Roland Schreiber, Eva Schrijver, Bernhard Schumann, Ulrich Schwabe, Valentine Seyfarth, Hamdi Shika, Ralf Sieber, Mira Siefken, Deborah Skoluda, Daniel Spreier, Viola Spurk, Ruth Stang, Ursula Stengel, Claudia Strahl, Niclas von Taboritzki, Georg Taxhet, Jan Tenbücken, Martin Terber, Maximilian Timmermann, Julia Tonn, Ria Unverzagt, Jan Volkmann, Lars Wagner, Malin Walleser, Sascha Walter, Stefan Weber, Ulrich Weingärtner, Simon Weins, Doris Weitz, Oliver Wenz, Gordon Werneburg, Tim Wessel, Robert Wetzels, Annabelle Wick, Costa Wild, Christian Winkler, Michaela Wippermann, Vera Witteck, Meike Wittrock, Steffen Wurzbacher, Zhen Xu, Inci Yilmaz, Dirk Zaloga, Mechtild Zeich, Michael Ziehl, Max Zielhardt, Henning Ziepke, Fabian Ziltz, Jörg Ziolkowski, Robert Zöllner

DREIUNDZWANZIG FRAGEN
TWENTY-THREE QUESTIONS

Ulf Meyer (UM) Was bedeutet das Kunstwort „ASTOC" – im Wortsinn und im übertragenen Sinn?

Peter Berner (PB) Das Büro wurde Anfang der 1990er Jahre zusammen mit unseren niederländischen Partnern gegründet. Das Wort ASTOC steht für „Architektur, Stadtentwicklung und Immobilienconsulting" und es beschreibt nach wie vor, was wir tun: Wir beschäftigen uns mit ganz unterschiedlichen Aufgaben in Architektur und Städtebau.

UM Welche Rolle spielt Kees Christiaanse für ASTOC?

Markus Neppl (MN) Für uns war Kees jemand, der das personifizierte, was wir in unserer Ausbildung in Deutschland vermisst haben. Für ihn gibt es keine Grenze zwischen den Kategorien Architektur und Städtebau. Wir sind ihm 1989 in Hamburg auf dem Bauforum über den Weg gelaufen, kurz nachdem er bei OMA ausgeschieden war. Das war der richtige Zeitpunkt für die Gründung eines zweiten Büros neben KCAP in Rotterdam. Es ging uns nicht um den Import/Export von Planungskultur, sondern um gemeinsames Lernen und Arbeiten. Kees hat unseren Horizont damals extrem geweitet. Die Niederländer gehen anders an die Aufgabe heran und sind auch anders organisiert.

Ulf Meyer (UM) What does the invented term "ASTOC" stand for, both in its literal and metaphorical sense?

Peter Berner (PB) The office was founded at the beginning of the nineteen-nineties together with our Dutch partners. The term ASTOC stands for "architecture, urban development, and real estate consulting". It continues to be appropriate for what we do: taking up different challenges within architecture and urban development.

UM What role does Kees Christiaanse play for ASTOC?

Markus Neppl (MN) For us, Kees is somebody who personified the things that we had missed during our education in Germany. For him, there is no boundary between the categories of architecture and urban planning. We bumped into him for the first time at the Bauforum in Hamburg in 1989, just after he had left OMA. The time was right to found a second office, apart from the existing KCAP in Rotterdam. We were not concerned with the import/export of planning culture, but rather with joint learning and working. Kees immensely broadened our horizons at the time. The Dutch have a different approach to tasks and are also organized differently.

We continue to have a good exchange of thoughts and ideas with Kees. At the same time, we decided not to wear ourselves out in too many joint projects, but rather work more intensively together on a select few tasks.

Wir haben mit Kees nach wie vor einen guten Austausch, haben aber beschlossen, dass wir uns nicht in zu vielen gemeinsamen Projekten verschleißen, sondern an ausgewählten Aufgaben eng zusammenarbeiten wollen.

UM Im Untertitel nennt sich Ihr Büro „Architects and Planners". Der Begriff schließt im Englischen jedoch den Städtebau gar nicht mit ein, „Planners" steht nur für die zweidimensionale Planung. Betrachten Sie Städtebau nicht als eine dreidimensionale Kunstform?

Oliver Hall (OH) Zwischen der architektonisch und der planerisch geprägten Denkweise gibt es leider traditionell einen großen Abstand. Beim Planen spielt die Zeit eine große Rolle und in der Architektur das Objekt und der Raum. Dazwischen klafft eine große Lücke. Die versuchen wir mit unserer Arbeit und Erfahrung zu überbrücken.

UM War Architektur zuletzt zu objektorientiert? Klassische Architekten beschäftigen sich bisweilen – ein wenig Abstandsgrün ausgenommen – nicht mit dem Umfeld ihrer Gebäude.

AK Das stimmt, wenn man sieht, was die reine Architektur ohne Erwägung von städtebaulichen Gesichtspunkten hervorgebracht hat. Bei der aus den 1950er Jahren stammenden Siedlung am Buchheimer Weg in Köln beispielsweise haben wir uns mit der Neugestaltung einer ganzen Siedlung beschäftigt. Es galt, eine Reihe von typischen Problemen dieser Siedlungsform zu beheben.

UM Die Sanierung von Wohnsiedlungen aus der Nachkriegszeit ist ein riesiges Thema. Damit öffnen Sie die Büchse der Pandora, denn jede (west-)deutsche Stadt ist voll mit welkenden 1950er-Jahre-Bauten.

PB Das ist richtig. Bei der Sanierung von Wohnsiedlungen aus der Nachkriegszeit sind jedoch ökologische, ökonomische und soziale Aspekte gleichzeitig zu berücksichtigen. Am Buchheimer Weg waren die Gebäude in einem sehr schlechten Zustand. Sie nur energetisch zu sanieren, wäre selbst mit den Fördergeldern, die man dafür hätte in Anspruch nehmen können, nicht rentabel gewesen. Daher entschied sich der Bauherr für einen Neubau der Siedlung.

UM Ist es vielleicht kein Zufall, dass Ihr Büro niederländische Wurzeln hat? Haben die Niederländer das Zusammendenken von Architektur und Stadt als Erste so klar gesehen und betrieben?

OH Die Unterscheidung zwischen einem Architekten und einem Städtebauer gibt es in Holland nicht. Jeder Architekt oder Landschaftsarchitekt definiert sich von jeher auch als Urbanist.

UM Ist ASTOC da, wo es sein will, angekommen? Oder wo will das Büro in fünf Jahren stehen?

Ingo Kanehl (IK) Beim Städtebau und der Planung stehen wir bei vielen Fragestellungen noch am Anfang. Verschiedene Projekte versuchen wir noch weiter zu durchdenken. Bei der HafenCity zum Beispiel gab es einen Wettbewerb. Danach ging man davon aus, dass der Plan fertig ist und nun alles gebaut werden könne. Nach der Planung fängt die Arbeit für uns aber erst an. Wir haben häufig noch große Probleme, unsere Auftraggeber von den Vorteilen einer langfristigen Projektbegleitung zu überzeugen.

UM Die Honorarordnung sieht ihre Leistungen gar nicht vor?

IK Genau, nach dem Masterplan und dem B-Plan gibt es meist einen völligen Personalwechsel. Wir können mittlerweile an einer Reihe von Projekten nachweisen, dass die Weiterbearbeitung für alle Vorteile hat. Die Vertreter von Städten und Gemeinden wie auch die Projektentwickler und Grundstückseigentümer haben viel schneller Sicherheit. Dabei muss es immer einen „inneren Kern" von Personen innerhalb eines Projekts geben. Bei der HafenCity Hamburg zum Beispiel besteht dieser „Kern" aus drei Teilen, dem Chef der Entwicklungsgesellschaft, dem Oberbaudirektor der Stadt Hamburg und dem Masterplaner – und dies schon seit zwölf Jahren.

UM Dafür bedarf es Geduld und Konsistenz?

MN Städtebau wird von vielen als das Umsetzen von Einzelinteressen angesehen. Dafür brauche ich lediglich neutrales Planungsrecht. Die Einzelinteressen können jedoch nur ausbalanciert werden, wenn die Planer präsent und vertreten sind. In Hamburg zum Beispiel vertritt der Oberbaudirektor Jörn Walter die planerischen Interessen der Stadt, während Jürgen Bruns-Berentelg als Vorsitzender der Geschäftsführung der HafenCity Hamburg GmbH die ökonomische Verantwortung hat. Wir agieren zwischen diesen Positionen und versuchen stets planerisch die Gegensätze zu überwinden.

UM Brauchen Sie stets Bauherren, die ihr Verständnis einer langfristigen Projektbegleitung haben und teilen?

UM The subtitle of your office reads "Architects and Planners". The English term "planners", however, does not include urban development, as the term seems to denote two-dimensional planning only. Don't you perceive urban development as a three-dimensional art form?

Oliver Hall (OH) Traditionally there has unfortunately been a large gap between architectural and planning mindsets. In planning, time plays a major role while in architecture it's the object and space. There lies a huge gap in between. It is this gap that we are trying to bridge with our work and experience.

UM Has architecture been too object-oriented in recent times? It seems to be standard practice among architects not to become too involved with designing the surroundings of their buildings, excepting the token inclusion of some minor and generic greenery.

AK That's true, especially when considering what so-called "pure" architecture that excludes urban planning aspects has produced. For the project of the housing complex at Buchheimer Weg in Cologne, dating from the fifties, we took on the challenge of completely redesigning an entire housing complex. The task was to rectify a series of problems associated with this type of residential development.

UM The redevelopment of post-war residential complexes has become a critical issue today. By engaging with this issue, you may seem to be opening Pandora's box since every (West-) German city is full of fading old buildings from the fifties.

PB Yes, that's right. However, the redevelopment of post-war housing complexes requires simultaneous attention to ecological, economic and social aspects. The buildings at Buchheimer Weg had been in a very bad shape. It would just not have been feasible to merely renovate them in energy terms, even considering the amount of financial aid which could have been provided. Therefore, the client decided to go for a complete new construction of the housing complex.

UM Is it true that your firm's Dutch roots are more than just a coincidence? Was it, indeed, the Dutch who were the first to clearly think about and implement architecture and city planning as joint disciplines?

OH In the Netherlands, there is no distinction between an architect and an urban planner. Every architect or landscape architect has always understood him-/herself to also be a city planner.

UM Has ASTOC reached the goal it set out to reach? Where does the office want to be in five years?

Ingo Kanehl (IK) In the areas of urban development and planning we are still at the beginning. We are trying to think through various projects. There was, for instance, a competition for the HafenCity. After that was over and the proposals had been submitted, the assumption was that the planning proposals were really all that was crucially needed to start thinking about construction. However, it is only following the planning stage that the real work for us begins. We frequently have great difficulty convincing our clients of the benefits of long-term project supervision.

UM Doesn't the fee schedule honor your services in this regard?

IK In most cases there is a complete change of expertise once the master-plan and the so-called development plan are completed. We are, however, in the meanwhile able to prove from a number of projects that the continuity of expertise and staff has benefits for all concerned. Security can be provided much more quickly to the representatives of cities and communities, as well as to project developers and property owners. In doing so, there should always be an "inner core" of persons working within a project. In the HafenCity project in Hamburg, for example, this "core" consists of three parts: the head of the development company; the senior construction manager of the city of Hamburg; and the master-planner. This has been the case for twelve years already.

UM Does this engagement require much patience and consistency?

MN Many view urban planning as an exercise in pushing through their own vested interests. This does not, however, require much more than a type of neutral planning law. Vested interests can nevertheless only be kept in check by planners who are actually present and represented at all times. In Hamburg, for example, it is the senior construction manager, Jörn Walter, who represents the planning interests of the city while Jürgen Bruns-Berentelg, as chairman of the management board of the HafenCity Hamburg GmbH is responsible for

MN Die Bauherren sind nicht das Problem, sondern es ist unsere Aufgabe, herauszufinden, wie wir die Ziele erreichen können. Wir wollen keine Bauherren austauschen. Die jeweilige Stadt, die Politik, muss bereit sein, die Rolle des „inneren Kerns" einzunehmen. Oft will sie sich jedoch aus dieser Verantwortung zurückziehen. Treten die Kommunen als Bittsteller auf, die den Investor ganz lieb um etwas bitten müssen, oder als selbstbewusste Städte, die eigene Vorstellungen von ihrer Entwicklung haben?

UM Das klingt verheerend. Entsteht durch den Rückzug der Politik ein Vakuum, das sie füllen können?

IK Wir stehen dazwischen. Wir sind nicht Träger des Planungsrechts und auch kein Bauherr. Wir sind mit weißen und roten Fahnen zwischen den Fronten unterwegs.

UM Ist Städtebau in der Summe eher Moderation als Entwurf?

IK Das glaube ich nicht. In der perspektivischen Entwicklung von Krankenhaus- und Hochschulstandorten tauchen beispielsweise jetzt Fragen auf, die sich aus der wachsenden nationalen und internationalen Konkurrenz dieser Institutionen ergeben. Zudem stellt sich die Frage, welche Potenziale diese Standorte über die reine Forschung hinaus bieten. Wie können diese Nutzungen Teil einer urbanen Stadtlandschaft werden?

OH Wir sind zwar ein Architekturbüro mit städtebaulicher Expertise, aber manchmal werden offene Fragestellungen aus anderen Disziplinen an uns herangetragen, wie zum Beispiel für den Kreis Höxter in Westfalen. Zahlreiche landwirtschaftlich geprägte Regionen haben ein Problem mit zu vielen Wirtschaftswegen, die instand gehalten und regelmäßig erneuert werden müssen. Für den Kreis Höxter haben wir ein sogenanntes „strategisches Straßen- und Wirtschaftswegekonzept" erstellt. Dabei ging es um insgesamt rund 4300 Kilometer Straßen und Wege, was allein aufgrund der Datenmenge eine planerische Herausforderung war. Herausgekommen ist dabei eine weitreichende Entscheidungsgrundlage für die betroffenen Kommunen des Kreises, in welche landwirtschaftlichen Wege investiert werden muss. Anstatt ständig Schlaglöcher zu flicken, werden in Zukunft die zur Verfügung stehenden Mittel an die richtigen Stellen gelenkt. Derartige Konzepte greifen weiter als die klassische Stadt- oder Verkehrsplanung, sie haben Pilotcharakter und sind übertragbar auf vergleichbare Räume und Problemstellungen.

UM Ist ein Büro mit sechs Köpfen wie ein Sack Flöhe? Ist es vielleicht gut so?

PB Als wir Anfang der 1990er Jahre das Büro gründeten, gab es Zweifel, weil alle drei Gründer, Hall, Neppl und ich, gleich alt sind und eine ähnliche Ausbildung haben. Das Büro hat sich jedoch stetig entwickelt und heute arbeiten wir mit sechs sehr unterschiedlichen Persönlichkeiten in der Geschäftsführung. Jeder hat bestimmte Talente und Fähigkeiten. Zu den drei Gründern kamen später noch drei Geschäftsführer hinzu: Andreas Kühn kümmert sich – neben vielen anderen Dingen – um wirtschaftliche Belange und Jörg Ziolkowski ist vor allem für die architektonischen Realisierungen zuständig. Ingo Kanehl macht das parallel im Städtebau.

UM ASTOC sucht auch die Nähe zur akademischen Welt?

MN Ich bin seit zwei Jahren und für weitere zwei Jahre Dekan an der Fakultät für Architektur am KIT in Karlsruhe. Darüber hinaus bin ich in vielen Preisgerichten und im Gestaltungsbeirat in Tübingen tätig. Kollegen sind nicht nur Konkurrenten. Diese Haltung versuche ich auch an der Fakultät zu kultivieren. Es fängt in der Hochschule an. Muss man nicht auch den folgenden Generationen klarmachen, dass sie nur dann gesellschaftlich und ökonomisch Erfolg haben können, wenn es Zusammenhalt gibt? Wenn die neue Generation zu Individualisten, die nur auf sich bezogen sind, erzogen wird, dann sind darin die Probleme des Berufsstandes begründet. Wenn jeder seine eigene Ästhetik hat, und sich jeder hinter seiner Tür sein eigenes Weltbild zimmert, dann können wir auf der architektonischen Ebene nicht mehr diskutieren. Man muss überlegen, wie Gebäude nebeneinander stehen können in der Stadt. Das hat mit dem Selbstverständnis der Architekten zu tun.

UM ASTOC ist …

MN … ein Unternehmen, das Raum bietet. Es ist nicht wie klassische Unternehmen von oben nach unten oder horizontal organisiert, sondern es ist ein Raum, den wir uns geschaffen haben. Wir sind jedoch keine passiven Dienstleister, die einfach nur ihre Aufgabe erfüllen. Es hat sich bewährt, sich nicht nur über ästhetische oder ökonomische Fragen zu definieren, sondern als aktiver Partner. Wir wollen immer zwei Schritte vor den Anderen sein und den

economics. We operate in between these positions and always try to bridge contradictions in terms of planning.

UM Do you always require clients who share your understanding of long-term project supervision?

MN The clients are not the problem. It is, rather, our job to ascertain how best to arrive at our goals. We don't want to exchange clients. Each city, coupled with effective public policy, ought to be ready to take on the role of an "inner core". In most cases, however, cities and the field of politics shy away from this responsibility. I ask why the municipalities so desperately want to make themselves appear as petitioners who have to always kindly ask investors for favors, rather than choosing to appear as self-confident cities with a clear understanding of their future development.

UM That sounds disastrous. Does the withdrawal of politics create a vacuum which you can fill?

IK We stand in an in-between position. We are neither the bearers of planning law nor are we the clients. We move between the lines that seem to be drawn.

UM Does urban planning amount to moderation rather than designing?

IK I don't think so. For instance, when we place the issue of the development of hospital and university sites in perspective, questions begin to surface that originate from the fact that these institutions are engaged in increasing national and international competition. Moreover, there is the question of what potential these locations offer beyond pure research and how these new uses can become part of a cityscape, for example.

OH Although we are an architecture firm with urban planning expertise, questions from other disciplines are sometimes posed to us, as was the case with the district of Höxter in Westfalen, for instance. Many predominantly agricultural regions have a problem with the fact that too many economic arteries run through them that all need to be regularly maintained and renovated. For the Kreis (district) Höxter, we developed a so-called "strategic economic arteries and roads concept" which included a total of around 4,300 kilometers of roads and tracks, representing a rather special planning challenge, just considering the amount of data that was included.

The result was a far-reaching basis for decision-making for the concerned municipalities of the Kreis to ascertain which agricultural routes needed investment. Instead of constantly fixing potholes, the available funds will, in future, be allocated to the right places. Concepts such as these go much further than classic urban or traffic planning proposals. They represent pilot projects and can serve as models for other similar spaces and problems.

UM Is running an office with six heads somewhat like herding cats? Is it perhaps an exemplary thing to do?

PB When we founded the office at the beginning of the nineties, there were certain doubts because all three founders, i.e. Hall, Neppl and myself, were the same age and had had a similar education. The office has, however, steadily developed and matured, and today we work with six very diverse personalities in senior management. Each one of us has specific talents and skills. The three founders were later joined by three managing directors: Andreas Kühn is in charge of economic concerns, among other things, and Jörg Ziolkowski is responsible for architectural implementation, in particular, and Ingo Kanehl likewise for the area of urban planning.

UM Does ASTOC also want to be associated with the world of academia?

MN For two years now, I have been Dean at the Faculty of Architecture at KIT in Karlsruhe, and will serve for another two years. I am also part of several juries and of the board of design in Tübingen. Colleagues are not just competitors. This is an understanding that I am trying to cultivate at the faculty too. It all starts at university. Is it not our responsibility to make amply clear to coming generations that they will only be socially and economically successful if they choose the path of cohesion and solidarity? If the new generation is brought up to become individualists who are only concerned with themselves, the profession and much else suffers. If everyone has their own aesthetics and begins to craft their own individual worlds view behind closed doors, we will cease to be able to discuss things on an architectural level. We have to think how exactly buildings can meaningfully stand next to each other in the context of the city. This has to do with the way architects perceive their professional challenges.

Takt angeben. Unsere besten Projekte sind die, in denen wir den Takt angeben und den Auftraggeber und die Öffentlichkeit überzeugen.

UM Ist ASTOC dann am besten und am glücklichsten, wenn sie ein Projekt von der Vogelperspektive bis zur Türklinke bearbeiten kann? Oder funktionieren Architektur und Städtebau auch als Selbstzweck?

OH Das kommt auf das Projekt an. Manche Projekte nehmen eine ungewöhnliche Wendung, die der Auftraggeber vielleicht vorher gar nicht formuliert hat. Einmal sind wir gebeten worden, in Solingen eine Bushaltestelle zu planen, herausgekommen ist aber eine Klärung der verkehrsstrukturellen Fragestellungen. Es war wichtig, als Architekt das Projekt zu vertreten und nicht nur als Verkehrsplaner. Es hat zwar lange gedauert, aber als alle überzeugt waren, bekam das Projekt eine besondere Dynamik.

Jörg Ziolkowski (JZ) Das führt in der architektonischen Ausführung dazu, dass die Projekte alle sehr individuell sind.

UM Sucht ASTOC denn eine Handschrift?

JZ Die Entwürfe entstehen aus dem Dialog mit dem Ort, dem Bauherren und der Aufgabe. Das ist unsere Handschrift, aber nicht, dass wir immer Naturstein verwenden oder Quadratraster.

UM Ich finde das stark, aber die Medien hassen so etwas.

OH Bei jedem Wettbewerb und jeder neuen Aufgabe müssen die Fragestellungen erst mal auf den Tisch. Der Fokus liegt dann zunächst nicht auf der Handschrift, sondern auf der Lösung eines Problems. Wenn man einen Entwurf angeht, muss man ein Problem definieren auf der begrifflichen Ebene. Sonst sind Entwürfe nur eine Reaktion einer Person auf einen Ort. Das ist mir viel zu wenig. Wenn man das nicht tut, bekommt man Abgüsse von Dingen, die in den Medien verbreitet werden. Für uns ist es wichtig, dass jeder seine Handschrift hat, denn man kann aus seiner Haut ja nicht heraus. Jeder bringt etwas mit und das muss auf den Tisch. Dann geht es aber darum, das zu neutralisieren und zu lösen, weil wir uns weiterentwickeln wollen.

AK Dadurch haben wir dann eine Stabilität in der Realisierung. Beim Buchheimer Weg zum Beispiel liegt der Fokus nicht auf aufwendigen Details oder teuren Materialien. Um den Neubau der Siedlung als öffentlich geförderten Wohnungsbau realisieren zu können, musste weder das Baurecht geändert noch die technische Infrastruktur neu angelegt werden. Der Entwurf basiert auf einem variierten Typengebäude. Trotz der Wiederholungen ist das Konzept vielfältig und den unterschiedlichen Bedingungen angepasst.

UM Fühlt sich ein Projekt anders an, wenn ASTOC es schon städtebaulich erdacht hat oder wenn ein Auftrag als Hochbauentwurf ins Haus kommt?

JZ Nein, denn alle unsere Entwürfe haben einen wichtigen stadträumlichen Aspekt. Unsere Gebäude treffen in den Außenräumen sehr differenzierte Aussagen. Die Kubaturen kommen oft aus den städtebaulichen Rahmensetzungen und ziehen sich wie ein roter Faden durch die Projekte, der uns leitet und uns hilft. Insofern dient der Städtebau als Wahrnehmung des Stadtraums auch bei den Hochbauprojekten.

IK Ich finde es momentan sehr viel schwieriger, auf der städtebaulichen Ebene eine Aussage zu machen als auf der architektonischen. Je mehr wir in die Umsetzung von städtebaulichen Ideen kommen, desto weniger unbefangen sind wir zum Beispiel bei Wettbewerben. Oft werden Wettbewerbe nach Kriterien entschieden, die gar nicht wesentlich sind. Denn die einzige bohrende Frage bei einem städtebaulichen Entwurf ist die Erschließung. Die Erschließung mit allen Medien ist entscheidend für die Kosten. Man muss genau wissen, wo sie hinkommt. Es geht um eine Phasierung, Erschließung und Nutzungsvorgabe. Andere Aspekte werden bei der Ausarbeitung des B-Plans ohnehin wieder neutralisiert.

UM Werden ästhetische und gesellschaftliche, politische Fragestellungen im Entwurfsprozess gleichwertig behandelt?

JZ Ein Schweizer Kollege hatte ein Bild des Projekts am Buchheimer Weg auf unserer Webseite gesehen und fand es unmöglich. Er fand die Zäune, den Putz und die Müllräume hässlich. In der Architektenschaft kommen wir da in den ästhetischen Diskurs und der verbietet all das. Als ich ihm sagte, zu welchem Budget und zu welchen Bedingungen wir das Projekt gebaut haben, da wurde er ganz still. Aber die Architekturdebatte blendet diese Themen aus. Das finde ich verantwortungslos. Ästhetisch ist das Projekt gut, aber natürlich beschränkt. Es ist nicht Mainstream, solche Projekte zu bauen. Das reizt uns.

UM Please complete the following statement: ASTOC is…

MN …an enterprise that offers space. It is not organized hierarchically or horizontally in the classic way. Rather, it represents a space which we have created for ourselves. We are not, however, passive service providers who simply go about completing a particular task. We have proven that it makes a big difference to be an active partner and to not just define ourselves in relation to aesthetic or economic concerns alone. We always want to be two paces ahead of others, and want to lead the way. Our best projects are those where we lead the way and where we are able to convince the client and the public.

UM Is ASTOC at its best and happiest when it is free to design everything from the macro-scale of a building down to the micro-scale of door handles? Does architecture and urban planning also function as a more limited end in itself?

OH That depends on the project. Some projects make unusual twists and turns that the client may possibly not have foreseen in the beginning. Once we were asked to plan a bus stop in Solingen, but the final result was a clarification of questions relating to transport structures. It was important to represent the project as architects and not just as traffic planners. It may have taken a long time, but once everyone was convinced, the project developed its own special dynamics.

Jörg Ziolkowski (JZ) In terms of the realization of architecture, this means that all projects are very distinct.

UM Is ASTOC looking for a signature style?

JZ Our designs are created by engaging in a dialog with the place, the client, and the brief. This can be taken to be our signature style. We don't, however, believe in always using natural stone or planning a square grid, for example.

UM I find this laudable, but the media seem to hate approaches like this.

OH In every competition and for every new task, the questions have to be formulated first. Initially, the focus doesn't lie on finding a signature style but on finding solutions for a particular problem. The design process starts out by defining a problem on the conceptual level. Otherwise, designs merely end up representing the subjective reaction of a particular person to a particular place. That's not sufficient and may only result in casting and recasting stuff that's spread by the media. At the same time, all of us are what we are and we want to acknowledge this. That's why it is important that each one of us doesn't feel guilty about having his own signature style. Every person makes his/her own contribution which then also becomes the subject of collective debate within the practice, where, in a second step, things are neutralized and solved. We always want to continue developing and refining ourselves.

AK This gives us a sense of stability during realization processes. In the Buchheimer Weg project, for instance, the focus didn't lie on complicated details and expensive materials. In order to newly build the housing complex as a publicly-funded housing development, it was not necessary to change building law, or to renew the technical infrastructure. The design is based on a modified building typology. In spite of the repetitions, the concept is flexible, to allow it to be applied to different conditions as they may be found.

UM Does it make a difference, if a building project has already seen prior involvement by ASTOC in its urban planning and development, compared to working on pure building assignments only?

JZ No, all our designs incorporate an important urban space aspect. The open spaces of our buildings make a variety of statements. The outer shapes are often derived from existing urban planning guidelines and conditions and run through the projects like a thread, guiding and helping us. As such, urban planning in its function as perception of urban space does play a role even for pure building assignments.

IK Currently, I find it much harder to make a meaningful statement on the urban planning level than on the level of architecture. The more we get involved with the realization of urban planning ideas, the less impartial we become in competitions, for example. Often competitions are decided by criteria that are not at all essential. For the only really pressing issue in an urban design is that of access. The way access to all the elements in a given situation is planned and implemented is crucial for the costs. It is important to know where and how to arrange access. This is all about phasing, access and utilization specifications. The other aspects are anyway neutralized during the formulation of the development plan.

UM Können auch andere Büros, was ASTOC kann?

MN Jeder Architekt gibt vor, auch den Städtebau zu beherrschen, und jeder Städtebauer sagt, Hochbau sei für ihn auch kein Problem. Aber es ist oft keine Substanz dahinter.

AK Auf dem Papier gibt es viele, die das tun, was wir tun. Wir sind in einer Gruppe von sehr guten Büros. Oft stehen wir in Konkurrenz, aber gelegentlich kooperieren wir auch mit anderen.

JZ Das Arbeiten in Konsortien oder Arbeitsgemeinschaften hat bei uns eine lange Tradition. Den Masterplan für die Hamburger Hafencity und die drei Gebäude im Holzhafen bearbeiten wir gemeinsam mit Kees Christiaanse. Für den Neubau der Hochschule Ruhr West in Mühlheim haben wir uns mit HPP zusammengeschlossen. Nicht nur bei uns im Haus scheint sich die klassische Abgrenzung, was ein Architekt zu tun hat, aufzulösen.

UM Ist der „Zoom" vom großen zum kleinen Maßstab essenziell für ASTOC?

PB Ja, letztlich entscheidend ist das realisierte Gebäude und nicht der städtebauliche Plan. Deutsche Architekten haben in der Welt ein gutes Image. Aber nach Deutschland kommt sehr wenig zurück. Wir müssen die Dinge, die sich global verändern, reflektieren und dazu eine Haltung entwickeln. Das Bauen in der Schweiz war für uns wichtig, weil wir etwas dort lernen wollten. Dasselbe gilt für die Niederlande. Wir wollen nicht nur exportieren. Wir wollen den Blick nach außen kultivieren. Wir wollen unser Know-how dort hinbringen, aber uns auch beeinflussen lassen, um unsere eigene Entwicklung anzufeuern. So haben wir den Weg in die Niederlande damals auch verstanden.

UM Vielen Dank für das Gespräch.

UM Are aesthetic, social, and political issues treated equally during the design process?

JZ A Swiss colleague once saw a picture of the Buchheimer Weg project on our website and did not like it at all. He thought the fences, the plaster and the garbage collection space were ugly. This brings us to the issue of aesthetic discourse within the architectural community which seems to ban the aesthetics we engage in. When I told him what the budget of the project had been and under what conditions we had built the project, he stopped criticizing it. The architectural debate blanks out these issues. I find that irresponsible. Aesthetically speaking, the project is good, but limited, of course. It is not considered mainstream to build such projects. This is what appeals to us.

UM Are other firms also capable of doing what ASTOC does?

MN Every architect claims to also be a master of urban planning, and every urban planner says that designing buildings is not a problem for him/her. Very often, however, there is very little substance behind these claims.

AK On paper there are many people and firms who do what we do. We are in the company of very proficient firms. Frequently we compete with each other, but occasionally we also cooperate with others.

JZ Working in consortia and in joint work groups has a long tradition within our firm. In the master-plan project for the HafenCity in Hamburg and for the three buildings at the Timber Docks we work together with Kees Christiaanse. We are collaborating with HPP for the new building of the University of Applied Sciences Ruhr West in Mühlheim. It's not just us who are suspending conventional preconceptions of what it is that an architect does.

UM Is "zooming in" from a large scale to the small essential for ASTOC?

PB Yes, what finally counts is the realized building and not the urban plan. German architects are well-respected around the world. But very little actually resonates back to Germany. We have to reflect global changes and need to develop a meaningful stance in relation to them. Building in Switzerland was important for us because we went there to learn something. The same applies to the Netherlands. We don't want to merely export things. We want to cultivate our perception of what lies beyond. We want to bring our know-how to other places but also be influenced by them ourselves, so that our own development is encouraged. This is also how we perceived our Dutch period at the time.

UM Thank you very much for this conversation.